Why Margaret Fuller Ossoli is Forgotten

Why
Margaret Fuller Ossoli
is Forgotten

by Laurie James

*A True Account—typical of how famous women
have been buried in history*

Volume 2
in a series on the life and work of
Margaret Fuller Ossoli (1810-1850)

Golden Heritage Press, Inc.
New York

1988

Cover Designer: Chris Hoogendyk, Coherent Graphics, Inc.

Designer and Compositor: Chris Hoogendyk, Coherent Graphics, Inc.

Set in ITC New Baskerville® 10/12 using a Macintosh™ computer and an Apple LaserWriter.® Title pages and cover output on a Linotronic® 100.

ITC New Baskerville is a registered trademark of International Typeface Corporation. Macintosh is a trademark of Apple Computer, Inc. Apple and LaserWriter are registered trademarks of Apple computer, Inc. Linotronic and Linotype are registered trademarks of Linotype Company.

Printed in the United States of America

Library of Congress Catalogue Card Number: 87-82465

ISBN 0-944382-01-0

to my mother

a creative woman who desired to achieve

MARGARET FULLER* once said that not one of her contemporaries could converse on a plane of equality with Rousseau and Goethe as she herself could.

Twentieth century scholar/biographer Perry Miller has admitted that, in historical perspective, she was probably right. Despite Miller's harsh criticism of her work and appearance, he thought there was truth in her remark: "Now I know all the people worth knowing in America and I can find no intellect comparable to my own."[1]

Yes, Margaret Fuller's scholarship and intellect was quicker, sharper, more realistic, more consistent, more humorous, more spontaneous than even that of Ralph Waldo Emerson, who was her intimate friend, mentor, biographer, and who achieved the highest of recognition.

She was fully cognizant of the dilemma in her arrogant egotism. She wrote: "In an environment like mine, what may have seemed too lofty or ambitious in my character was absolutely needed to keep the heart from breaking and enthusiasm from extinction."[2]

No matter how critics have judged her throughout a century and a half, her written words signify that she was a maker and definer of America's culture on a level to match that of Ralph Waldo Emerson.

---

*The name "Fuller" is used throughout this book in preference to "Ossoli" because this was her pen name and therefore the name by which Americans best knew her.

What Emerson was doing for men, she was doing for men *and women.*

Emerson was proffering the ideals of truth, divinity and harmony of nature, God and man. He called for self-reliance and individualism for men. He held up models of representative men: Plato, Socrates, Swedenborg, Montaigne, Shakespeare, Napoleon, Goethe.

Fuller, whose influence had inspired Emerson to select Goethe as a model, was proffering the same ideals of truth, divinity and harmony in nature, God and man *and woman.* She called for self-reliance and individualism for women. She held up the models of Sappho, Aspasia, Isis, Semiramis (legendary Assyrian queen who built Babylon), Countess Emily Plater (a Polish Joan-of-Arc heroine who joined the army), Elizabeth of England, Catharine of Russia, Mary Wollstonecraft (the English woman right's advocate), Madame de Staël (the French woman right's advocate), George Sand, Anglelina Grimke and many others.

Fuller's words were read by more people in the 1840's than Emerson's.

But the question is not who was better than who, but why has a significant person like Margaret Fuller been forgotten?

Fuller, dying at the age of forty in 1850, had earned a controversial reputation as being one of the most radical and intellectual persons in the English-speaking world. Her book and her dominating front page reviews and articles were read by all Americans who cared to keep up with the most current.

The first edition of her best and major and revolutionary work, *Woman In The Nineteenth Century,* (written in her early thirties) was sold out within a week, a reported 1500 copies,* in a day when 500-1000 copies was considered an average printing run. And after the publishers netted their costs and profits, she received $85. A second edition was issued, as well as an English edition.

Emerson, in order to publish and distribute 500 copies of his first and most major and revolutionary work, *Nature,* (written in his early thirties) paid for it himself, a method regarded as unfavorable at that time,** and he gave away many copies free to friends.

---

* Fifteen hundred was the number according to Horace Greeley.
** Fuller had considered paying for the publication of her book, but dismissed the idea, writing to friend William Henry Channing that both he and Horace Greeley "would not think that the favorable way as to securing a sale." [3]

His book took over ten years to sell in the USA,* though in England it sold well.

Fuller was surprised her book sold so well. As she wrote to a friend, she would have been "satisfied if it moves a mind here and there...if an edition of a thousand is disposed of in the course of two or three years." Fuller's object in writing the book was "in no wise money," but "to be heard, that is enough"; nevertheless, she considered her share of $85 "the signet of success." [4]

Critics found much to denounce in Fuller's work, but it was so controversial that everyone talked about it, and it was in such demand that it was immediately pirated overseas—reprinted and sold without knowledge of or profit to the author, a common unfair practice at the time.

Emerson probably was indifferent to the fact that Fuller's book sold better than his, because his dictum always was "everything great and excellent in the world is in minorities." [5]

Emerson's book received some good reviews, but some critics and intelligentsia admitted they could not understand it, while most average run-of-the-street-persons never noticed it was available for buying. It was five years before English publishers considered *Nature* worthy of piracy.

I've been angered for years about Fuller's invisibility in textbooks. She is not awarded the space and respect that is given to our American geniuses such as Ralph Waldo Emerson. Her image has been grossly distorted.

We are deeply indebted to her. She was first American to write a book on equality for women and men. She laid the groundwork for our feminist movement.

She was one of our country's first woman journalists, one of the first to write a vivid book on the West, and the first woman to write for Horace Greeley's *New York Daily Tribune.*

She was first editor of *The Dial Magazine,* one of America's first literary journals.

She was first American female foreign correspondent, reporting on a revolutionary war under combat conditions.

She was one of our first literary critics and among the first to set standards for literary criticism. She was one of our first

---

* It was not until his last book, *The Conduct of Life,* was published in 1860 that Emerson enjoyed a popular sale—2500 copies sold within a few days.

translators and she introduced and promoted the writings of Goethe in this country.

She was one of the first to cover and call for social reforms of women's conditions in New York prisons and asylums.

Fuller was one of the first to start "Conversations" for women— what we would today call adult education or "rap" sessions. She raised consciousness as well as confidence and argued that women did have minds. Her innovative beliefs encompassed the revolutionary concept of higher education for women.

She established precedence by being first woman to set foot inside Harvard Library, then Gore Hall, one of the largest and best libraries in America.

As foreign correspondent, she sent Horace Greeley her European travel observations; she documented European social concerns such as conditions in coal mines. She interviewed and wrote about such literary luminaries as Thomas Carlyle, George Sand, Wordsworth, De Quincy. She covered the politics and action of the Italian Revolution of 1848 and dispatched some of the best eye-witness accounts Americans have ever been privileged to read.

In Rome she was named Regolatrice of the Hospital of the Fate Bene Fratelli on the Tiber Island, which had been established to aid the war wounded. Thus, Fuller pre-dates nursing reformers Florence Nightingale* who brilliantly re-organized military hospitals during the Crimean War of 1854, and Clara Barton who directed large-scale hospital relief operations during America's Civil War in 1864.

People called Margaret Fuller "arrogant," "pedantic," "aggressive," "ugly," "manly." Educated persons ridiculed her. Edgar Allen Poe, who printed that she was a genius, also called her an "ill tempered old maid." Many men and women felt threatened

---

* In Rome during the winter of 1847-8 Fuller met the 28 year-old Nightingale who was stopping for six months while on a European tour with friends. By this time Nightingale had had her call from God and knew that her life work was to be in nursing and public health. She had already compiled voluminous notes on hospital sanitary conditions. Nothing is known of what transpired during the visit between Nightingale and Fuller, but because of these facts it is interesting to speculate that their conversation centered on nursing and therefore Nightingale (ten years younger than Fuller) could have been influential in Fuller's decision to accept the post at the Tiber Island hospital set up for the war wounded. Nightingale left Rome just as Garibaldi entered...just as the city took up arms. It was a year later, April 1849, that Fuller became the Regolatrice of the Hospital of the Fate Bene Fratelli.

by her. When her book advocating equality appeared on the scene, her writing was labelled "absurd," "immoral," "scandalous." Fuller wrote a friend: "Abuse public and private is lavished upon its views, but respect expressed for me personally." [6]

From 1845 until she died she was a literary lioness in America and Europe.

Yet Fuller is not remembered today.

Emerson is remembered today and there is no question that a century after his death he is accorded a most revered rank as statesman of American thought, dean of American literature.

Fuller's threat or power over Emerson in death gave cause for him—along with others—to decide it was necessary to alter, censor, and destroy her letters and papers. Thus, he and other male editors (plus members of her own family) have held power over her and have controlled her reputation to this day.

Had Fuller lived another forty years, undoubtedly she would have far surpassed Emerson in solid achievement. Posterity would have been forced to ascribe to her a position of lasting fame. Emerson and other men would not have been able to tamper with her reputation as they did...Emerson mumbling the question: "Is Margaret Fuller worth a Memoirs?"

The great sage of Transcendentalism, Octavius B. Frothingham could never have climaxed a chapter on her by stating that eminent men remarked that "it was just as well so" that Fuller died at this early age because she might have caused agitation with "her lightning pen"....because "the conservatives were glad when (brave voices were) hushed by death..." and had "the priestess" survived, "she would have found a deserted shrine." [7]

How totally mistaken was this surmise, actually echoed by large numbers of persons at the time. How little they comprehended the totality of the tragic loss of Margaret Fuller, not to mention their lack of compassion—or should we say jealousy? Had she lived, once the wind had blown away the malicious rumors, Fuller would have been one of our country's major guides/spokespersons throughout the Civil War and for twenty or thirty years thereafter, as demonstrated by her intense, matured humanitarian involvement in the Italian Revolution.

In comparison, Emerson had almost 80 years to become a remembered figure and was not awarded posterity's citation until the last half of his life.

During the first half of his life, until about 1840-45, a few years before Fuller died, Emerson's reputation was largely confined to New England. Here he was considered radical, outside the church, different. His views were new, "far out", some called him "mad." The Rev. James Freeman Clarke, friend of Emerson's and Fuller's, is quoted to have said: "The majority of the sensible, practical community regarded him as mystical, as crazy or affected, or as an imitator of Carlyle, as racked and revolutionary, as a fool, as one who did not himself know what he meant." [8]

Emerson's new philosophy, named Transcendentalism, was generally unpopular. He was voted out of his church by his parishioners. He was ostracized from the traditionalist milieu of Harvard University (his alma mater) for many years. As touring lecturer, his audiences were comparatively small, averaging 250-300 persons in an age when front-rank lecturers were commanding 1000.* Emerson attracted the same audience over and over again. It was a select group made up, on the one hand, of some of the most erudite, cultivated and scholarly persons and, on the other hand, of young extremists. While some honored him as a great innovator and valued his words as "the signets of reality," as Margaret Fuller was later to write, [9] many others opposed his views. There was nothing concrete or logical to hold onto. One confused man deferred to his wife's opinion: "My wife says it is about the elevation of human nature, and so it seems to me."

Some educated persons laughed, some ridiculed. Some who had earlier defended him learned to disparage.** To many his philosophy seemed to promote pretension, self-admiration, and spiritual immorality. The majority considered it visionary, dreamy, or pantheistic. Some despaired his want of logic, the exaggeration of the intuitive powers. Oliver Wendell Holmes called his work "vague, mystic, incomprehensible, to most of those who call themselves commonsense people." [10] Someone joked that his essays could be read backward as well as forward because sentences were not connected. Emerson was lambasted for inadequacy, underdevelopment, living apart, for refusing to serve society.

---

* There was one exception: in England he managed to attract some audiences of 1000.

** George Ripley and other Brook Farmers, as well as Orestes A. Brownson.

It was after the Civil War that Emerson solidified his reputation as a popular revered world figure who was worthy of large quantities of space in history books. It was after the old generation of conservatives had passed from the scene, after the Transcendentalists and abolitionists had faded into new directions that his views became acceptable to a majority. Then Harvard honored him with the degree of L.L.D., made him an overseer and invited him to give another Phi Beta Kappa address. Though he never commanded the largest audiences or the highest fees on the popular lecture circuit, it was then that people flocked to hear him; it was then his books sold.

In stacking up Fuller's achievements, you must realize that she did what she did within a lifespan of forty years, and you must measure in the cultural barriers she struggled against.

In the early nineteenth century the code of conduct for women was more constrained than at any other point in American history. During the eighteenth century rural Colonial period all hands had been needed to maintain the life sustaining chores. Women did the spinning and churning; men brought in the harvest. Thus, women's contribution had been economically beneficial and women held some value and respect.

With the turn of the century and the process of urbanization and industrialism, the workplace shifted to the business world, and the largest share of the productive role was shouldered by men who alone earned the money away from the home. Women, who remained in the home, became more and more dependant on husbands to provide support.

The true nineteenth century woman succeeded admirably in becoming an "ornament" of the household. Social mores pressured women to learn from early childhood on to conform to the "cult of true womanhood." This has been best described in four nouns: purity, piety, submissiveness and domesticity. These strictures were not subjected onto Emerson.

By conforming, a true woman could expect security, and protection for life. In the home, she could exert a certain amount of power. From the pedestal she could expect to be put on, she could expect from the man she married a certain reverence or worship, certain courtesies and deference. But he would be her god, her salvation; she would listen to him and follow his directives.*

But this myth of true womanhood, which perpetuates even into our century, was all too often shattered for women frequently outlived their husbands and they often faced poverty because employment opportunities were limited, often just at a time when they had young children to raise. Typical cases: Sarah Margaret Fuller's mother, Margaret, and Ralph Waldo Emerson's mother, Ruth.

There were no occupations for the average woman other than teacher/governess, companion, shop saleslady, factory worker, midwife, nurse, dressmaker, lacemaker, servant, laundress, prostitute. There was the alternative of becoming a nun or a missionary and to join one of a handful of Catholic Sisters of Charities groups scattered throughout the world, that is, if the woman was aware of their existence.

Of these employments, teaching was generally considered the most attractive, though salary would be about half—or less than half—of what male teachers would earn, and a teacher or governess (or companion) might have to move away from home and friends for long periods.

You wouldn't want to choose to be a factory worker as often you would have to put in eighteen monotonous hour work days with your pay earning you a life impoverishment.

Seamstresses had to work night and day for an average of thirty-one to thirty-eight cents a day, and you really couldn't pay room and board for that. And it was disheartening because male clients invariably took their suits to male tailors who charged double or triple what their female counterparts charged.

Usually, the most destitute and uneducated women became nurses because they could not find employment elsewhere. Nurses were recruited from vagrant and criminal groups; they were drunkards, immoral characters, hardly what you would call reliable. Hospitals were death traps because of inadequate supplies, filth, vermin, overcrowded conditions. The dead were often left on the floor. There was no knowledge yet of antiseptic.

---

* In actuality, this standard could only be upheld in upper-middle-class or upper class families. Other women had to work. But since everyone knew that the home was where every woman aspired to be, it was assumed that she would be there just as soon as opportunity presented itself.

Emetics, purgatives, and bloodletting were the prevailing cures. Doctors had little training. Unsanitary surgical methods actually promoted the spread of disease. You took a shot of whiskey for an amputation. You did not birth your baby in a hospital.

To earn money some women were able to open small shops and some managed to run boarding houses, and some, whose husbands had died, took over the family business, if it were small and relatively independent, such as a print shop or farm. In the latter case, women often found themselves heaving manure.

A handful of women could find employment in the arts, acting, painting, dancing, and singing, as exemplified by Abby Hutchinson who with her two brothers comprised a self-taught travelling family troupe of choral singers that became quite popular.

Theater management and acting were careers that afforded women pay equal to that of male managers, but this was only for exceptionally strong women who could take the daily doses of harassment since female entrepreneurs and actresses were stigmatized by clergy and public as social outcasts, one level above prostitutes. It was many years before editor Horace Greeley would accept advertising from theaters in his *New York Tribune;* he only changed his mind after he concluded that people attended the theater whether or not there was newspaper advertising. Even top stars who could command professional respect and salary, like Charlotte Cushman, Anna Cora Mowatt, Mary Ann Duff, and Fanny Kemble, were not usually invited into society. Generally, it was around the theater districts that prostitutes plied their trade. Actresses performed largely in front of male audiences. Inside the theater, during intermission, there were certain rooms allocated for a gentleman's relaxation. Only on very special occasions under the best of circumstances did respectable ladies attend the theater—a place that excited the emotions and was considered detrimental to the feminine character.

Dancers were also considered immoral and one mother is reported to have preferred her daughter to be a domestic rather than a ballerina. Fanny Elssler was the top calibre exception.

Drawing and painting were "nice" if you dabbled in your home during spare moments and sold your work for the cost of paint or gave it away to friends, as Nathaniel Hawthorne's wife did. There were no schools in which women could train, no sales outlets.

Writing, editing and publishing were fields with decent pay-offs that were opening up to the exceptional few with appropriate talent and guts to stand against the tide since bluestockings were disparaged. Such domestic works as cookbooks were best sellers, as well as household hints, advice and etiquette books. Children's stories also did well. One or two women even wrote histories. A few women like Eliza Farrar, Lydia Maria Child, Maria Edgeworth (Irish), Anna Brownell Jameson (English), were able to succeed as writers—all of whom Fuller read, and Sarah Josepha Hale established her highly successful magazine, *Godey's Lady's Book* in 1827. In 1840 the mill women workers in Lowell, Massachusetts edited their own paper, *The Lowell Offering* for nine years, some of whose writers went on to important posts or became novelists.*

---

* Eliza Farrar wrote *The Young Ladies Guide*, an etiquette book. Maria Edgeworth wrote *Castle Rankrent* and other novels. Lydia Maria Child wrote more than fifty works, novels, *Hobomok, The Rebels, Philothea*, newspaper columns for the *Boston Courier*, children's books, and anti-slavery tracts, one called, *An Appeal to that Class of Americans Called Africans*. Catharine Maria Sedgwick wrote *A New-England Tale* (1822), *Redwood (1824)* and *Clarence* (1830). Anna Brownell Jameson wrote *Memoirs of Celebrated Female Sovereigns* and *Visits and Sketches at Home and Abroad*, and many other works. Sarah Josepha Hale wrote *Northwood* (1827), and was editor of *Godey's Lady's Book*, a magazine for women, and recorded the lives of 1700 women in *"Woman's Record, Sketches of all the distinguished women from the Creation to A.D. 1868."* Eliza Buckminster Lee, *Sketches of a New-England Village* and *Life of Jean Paul Frederic Richter;* Hannah Farnham Sawyer Lee, *Three Experiments of Living* (1837); Elizabeth Caroline Grey, *De Lisle: or, the Distrustful Man* (London, 1828); Anne Manning (anonymously) *Village Belles* (London, 1833); Hannah Adams wrote *Summary History of New England, The Truth and Excellence of the Christian Religion, The History of The Jews*. Mercy Otis Warren wrote *"A History of the Rise, Progress, and Termination of the American Revolution"* (1805). Mrs. Ross wrote *Hesitation, or To Marry or Not To Marry?* which Fuller read when she was nine. Eliza Lee Cabot Follen wrote *Sketches of Married Life* (1838). Maria Weston Chapman wrote poetry and articles, and the English poet Felicia Dorothea Hemans was popular in this country for *"Casabianca"* *("The boy stood on the burning deck.")* Other names and editors and writers of the day were Mrs. Kirkland, Mrs. Osgood, Mrs. Ellet, Mrs. Sigourney. In Vermont, Clarina Howard edited the *Windham County Democrat* from 1843-53; in Akron, Ohio, Rebecca Sanford edited *The True Kindred* ; in Pittsburgh, Pa, Jane Grey Swisshelm edited *The Pittsburgh Saturday Visitor*, established 1848; in Seneca Falls, New York, Amelia Bloomer edited and published *The Lily* in 1849, a temperance paper. In Milwaukee, Wisconsin, *Die Frauen Zeitung*, was edited by Mathilde Franceska Anneke in 1849; in 1850 Mrs. Prewett edited the *Yazoo Whig*, in Mississippi, and Mrs. Sheldon edited the *Dollar Weekly*. Julia Ward Howe and husband edited *The Commonwealth*, in 1851, devoted to emancipation of slavery. There were still others advocating abolition, temperance, and women's rights, but remembered best are

(Continued)

But the writing profession was risky for both men and women. While some women did make substantial amounts of money, most were underpaid and then they had to hand profits over to husband or father. The skillful, to earn a livelihood, had to resort to writing short pieces and verse or compile anthologies.

On the other hand, women were insatiable readers, and the field was daily enlarging to those who could fill the popular need of what today would be thought of as moralist-type tales concerning young women who somehow withstood and overcame adverse circumstances. Once Fuller tried her hand at the short story, but learned that fiction was not for her. The successful few sold to mass audiences and their books went through many printings. But these works by women have not been considered worth remembering, not worth chronicling as claiming a lasting effect on our literary heritage.

Most women who dared let their creative energies flow, other than in quilting or pie baking, suppressed or hid their output like Emily Dickinson, who lived later in the century, to whom most people today can relate because her name did become known— *but only after she died*—but most women of course never achieved fame. Their energies were not valued and their work is lost to us.

The full impact of the nineteenth century woman's position hits hard when you read the advice Nathaniel Hawthorne gave to his beloved wife in 1843. He was here trying to protect her from the pain and headache which had dominated her life:

> "Take care of thy little self, I tell thee. I praise Heaven for this snow and 'slosh,' because it will prevent thee from scampering all about the city, as otherwise thou wouldst infallibly have done. Lie abed late, sleep during the day, go to bed seasonably, refuse to see thy best friend if either flesh or blood be sensible of the slightest repugnance, drive all trouble from thy mind, and, above all things, think continually what an admirable husband thou hast!" [11]

The Una, begun by Paulina Wright Davis, 1953 in Providence, R. I., and *The Revolution*, started in New York by Susan B. Anthony, Elizabeth Cady Stanton and Parker Pillsbury in 1868.

Here is Ralph Waldo Emerson's opinion of women's sphere in society which he freely inserted into his biography on Margaret Fuller:

> A woman in our society finds her safety and happiness in exclusions and privacies. She congratulates herself when she is not called to the market, to the courts, to the polls, to the stage, or to the orchestra. Only the most extraordinary genius can make the career of an artist secure and agreeable to her...a female politician is unknown. [12]

It was quite suitable for America's most popular, most eminent writer, Washington Irving, to write:

> As the vine, which has long twined its graceful foliage about the oak, and been lifted by it into sunshine, will, when the hardy plant is rifted by the thunder-bolt, cling round it with its caressing tendrils, and bind up its shattered boughs, so is it beautifully ordered by Providence that woman, who is the mere dependent and ornament of man in his happier hours, should be his stay and solace when smitten with sudden calamity, winding herself into the rugged recesses of his nature, tenderly supporting the drooping head and binding up the broken heart. [13]

Many nineteenth century Americans read a reprinted book by Englishman John Gregory called *A Father's Legacy to His Daughters,* which stated that girls did well if they remained silent when around others. "Wit is the most dangerous talent you can possess," he wrote, and "if you happen to have any learning, keep it a profound secret, especially from the men."

These ideas of women's position were embedded within the church and its teachings. In fact, in 1837 the General Association of Massachusetts Churches circulated the following pastoral letter to their member churches in response to the temperance and women's rights movements which were pushing women onto the platform of public awareness:

> The power of woman is her dependence, flowing from the consciousness of that weakness which God has given her for her protection, and which keeps her in those departments

of life that form the character of individuals, and of the nation...

We appreciate the unostentatious prayers and efforts of woman in advancing the cause of religion at home and abroad; in Sabbath-schools; in leading religious inquirers to the pastors for instruction...but when she assumes the place and tone of man as a public reformer, our care and protection of her seem unnecessary; we put ourselves in self defence against her; she yields the power which God has given her for her protection, and her character becomes unnatural. If the vine, whose strength and beauty is to lean upon the trellis-work, and half conceal its clusters, thinks to assume the independence and the overshadowing nature of the elm, it will not only cease to bear fruit, but fall in shame and dishonor into the dust. [14]

Such thinking echoes into our century. Emerson's 1915 biographer, Oscar W. Firkins wrote about the epitome of woman-hood when he referred to Emerson's second wife:

One feels in Mrs. Emerson the combination of an active force which could evoke for her husband all the conditions of a care-free and fruitful silence with 'wise passiveness,' capable of merging itself, when need was, in the very silence it had wrought. She satisfied two main needs of Emerson in his house-partner, tranquility and steadfastness. [15]

Margaret Fuller never could conform to the standard of womanhood.

It was the day and age when you didn't ask for a piece of chicken *breast*...when a lady did not *sweat*.

It was the day and age when Julia Ward Howe and other upper class ladies, honored with an invitation to a public dinner given for Charles Dickens during his American tour, had to remain in an adjoining room.

Genteel young women did not attend public lectures. They might carry a tune, play the harpsichord, do fancy embroidery, dance, have nice penmanship, swing corkscrew curls and long skirts on unpaved roads, but learned women were suspected of being heretics, trouble-makers.

Many grown women were illiterate, though as Margaret Fuller was growing up, total illiteracy was increasingly being regarded as not in the best interests of women or of their husbands.

Young men had had Harvard, Yale, and Princeton for over half a century plus other smaller colleges while young women had no comparative higher education. Boys regularly went to grammar schools, academies, seminaries, while girls, usually excluded, went to convents, or small local religious academies run by clergymen, or Quaker seminaries. If a liberal boys school admitted girls, the sexes were commonly separated. Most girls stayed home and received instruction from father and mother, but some advantaged girls had local tutors who were either young male undergraduates, badly educated spinsters or widows struggling to make ends meet, or persons who could not find better employment.

As for female "higher education," the advantaged went to segregated boarding or finishing schools with curriculums which included the domestic arts as well as instruction on how to find and keep a husband. Education ended somewhere between the ages of fourteen and sixteen or earlier, while advantaged boys continued in college until eighteen or twenty or longer, following a course of studies that enabled them to become professionals such as lawyers, clergymen, or doctors.

Women such as Margaret Fuller, Elizabeth Peabody, Julia Ward Howe, Elizabeth Cady Stanton, were able to read widely because their fathers and brothers had fine libraries and/or because their brothers brought their textbooks home. Howe, who stayed home in America while her brother travelled to Europe for an education, writes: "After my brother's return from Europe, I read such works of George Sand and Balzac as he would allow me to choose from his library." [16] She learned German by conversing with her brother who'd learned it in Germany and thus she was able to read Goethe's *"Faust,"* a book her father banned to her because he considered it wicked, which was the prevailing opinion.

Many really believed that higher education for women would interfere with having healthy babies.

Every young girl was assuredly acculturized to become married, for men did not favor intelligent women—mates who might usurp their superiority.

If a young woman grew up to recognize her intelligence and ability, she quickly learned to disclaim, to disparage, to apologize for it. Hannah Adams, one of our country's first female professional writers, who wrote *Summary History of New England, The Truth and Excellence of the Christian Religion, The History of The Jews* , called herself "a mere woman."

The brightest often excused giftedness by claiming it came, as a miracle, from God. Like Joan of Arc, Florence Nightingale heard a voice speak to her four separate times; she felt *called* to His service. Harriet Beecher Stowe claimed that an unseen power, God, wrote *Uncle Tom's Cabin.* Modest and devout Mary Lyon not only gave the credit to God for establishing the first woman's college in America, Mt. Holyoke Female Seminary, but also to *men* :

> It is desirable that the plans relating to the subject should not seem to originate with us, but with benevolent *gentlemen.* If the object should excite attention, there is danger that many good men will fear the effect on society of so much female influence and what they will call female greatness. [17]

Women were supposed to have charm and grace. Woe to those who were not beautiful.

Thus was Fuller damned.

None of the American men who saw and knew Fuller thought she was beautiful, including Ralph Waldo Emerson.

Everyone concurred that Henry David Thoreau was ugly but, no matter, his work was not judged by his appearance.

No matter that Caroline Healey Dall, who attended Fuller's Conversations, pointed out in a lecture: "She was more than beautiful. A sort of glow surrounded her and warmed those who listened." [18]

Octavius Brooks Frothingham, leading Transcendentalist writer, twelve years younger than Fuller, who probably never came face to face with her because otherwise he would have printed his experience, emphasized her non-beauty by making it an issue at the end of his chapter on her. His summation was typical of nineteenth century macho:

> She was not beautiful in youth, nor was she one of those who gain beauty with years. Her physical attractions were

of the kind that time impairs soon, and though she died at forty, her personal charm was gone. Intellect gave her what beauty she had, and they saw it who saw her intellect at play. [19]

Women were trained to please men, to be companions to men and to support, to enable their work. Women, when young, lived under the jurisdictions of their fathers, and when married, lived under the jurisdictions of their husbands, and in old age, often lived under the jurisdictions of their sons.

In contrast, nineteenth century boys were allowed the greatest of freedom—were made to feel they could attain any goal they worked for, even become president of the United States, and for them the double standard prevailed.

Public opinion and newspapers denounced women who in the smallest way tried to change the status quo. Organizations and institutions of all types were closed to women. Public speaking, for a woman—even speaking in a church*—was practically a sin. Women did not appear in "promiscuous" assemblies, that is in groups which mixed together the indiscriminate elements of the human race—in other words, in groups which included men unknown to individual women because, who knows, they might be of dubious character.

Ministers constantly preached the message that women should be in subjection to men, even though they depended on women's solid support, their dollar contributions, volunteer work, and the cultivation of their male family members to attend Sunday services. Forward congregations heatedly debated as to whether or not to allow women the privilege of singing, teaching, praying and preaching, and none could serve on vestry or board or be a representative at a meeting. The earliest female abolitionists found they not only had to speak out for the rights of slaves, but also for their own right of free speech.

Voting for women was prohibited, as was holding public office, while all white men, young or old, educated or uneducated, rich or poor, immigrant and foreign born who signed papers stating an intention to become citizens, had the vote and could hold public office.

---

* The exception was the Quaker religion, which permitted women to become ministers.

Yet if women owned property through inheritance or other means, they were taxed. Women could be prosecuted and convicted—but not with a trial by a jury of peers, for women were not permitted to serve on juries.

Women were trained to believe that they were above or outside the rude and rough world of public affairs; they could not understand the affairs of the world. Men protected them from all this ugliness, freed them from worry and responsibility. It was widely viewed that women did influence the thinking and votes of their husbands, fathers, and brothers.

Those aggressive women who did become politically involved to the great outrage of the majority—and these were largely those whose fathers, brothers and husbands were politicians—were limited to attending rallies, public meetings, and parades. They gathered petitions, travelled with a political father or husband, helped in his campaign, hosted events and dinners. Most women activated little political interest.

Marriage was considered the best lifestyle, but married women's indispensable enabling ministrations generated no salary, were devalued as less important than men's work.

The old law stated that wife and husband became one person, so legally the wife was submerged; she ceased to exist. As has been pointed out, she was dead. Thus, domestic happiness was thought to be ensured, just as it had been thought that women had no right to choose their religion, because there would be disagreement in the household if she differed from her mate. The usual reasoning was: "When the two heads disagree, who must decide?" The scriptures of St. Paul (unmarried) would be quoted: "man is head of the woman."

It was not unacceptable for a married woman, if her husband died, to wear black and to reclusively exclude herself from society for the rest of her life, as though dead herself, as in fact Nathaniel Hawthorne's mother and sisters did.

Wife and children, like slaves, were considered husband's property. If a woman brought money or property into the marriage, in almost every case, her husband was entitled to control her money or property as his own, as in fact Emerson controlled the income of both his wives. If wife had creditors, husband could collect. He could collect the earnings of the children; he could even sell the clothing and valuables of wife and children to pay his debts, as Susan B. Anthony's father did. A woman had no legal recourse if her husband spent the family income on liquor or, as Emerson did, on his personal interests. If she decided to leave her husband, he could use the law to bring her back. He could do with the children as he chose, place them in apprenticeships or under a guardian of his choosing; in fact, he would retain custody of the children in the rare case of divorce. A married woman could not sign a contract. She could not make a will without husband's consent. All she could ask of him, legally, was minimal support. If she died first, he was left, possessing all there was, the children left in his care. But if he died first, male relatives or strangers would assume authority, as happened in the case of Margaret Fuller. The house would often be assessed and sold, as happened in the case of Margaret Fuller. The children would often be entrusted to guardians, as would have happened to Fuller's younger brother and sister, had Fuller not fought against her uncle and gone to work as a teacher to earn the extra money needed for their support and education.

What women had was invisible power and control. A noble wife took care of her husband, protected him from his weaknesses and failures and made it appear to others that he was the superior. Her sacrifices, her repressions were supposed to give her life a focus, to make her an unsung heroine, a superior. This idea was promoted in novels and literature of the day. But this secret, which men supposedly did not know of, became a factor that separated husbands from wives. It helped to keep men and women distanced.

Marriage, in fact, deprived man and wife of many common interests. Limited to the home, her intellectual boundaries narrowed while his broadened as he worked in the "world." Husbands were set apart from women's sphere; in fact, they were bored by it, would find ways to escape it for periods of time, as indeed Ralph Waldo Emerson demonstrated. Qualities wives needed to develop were heart, purity, gentleness, humility, meekness, submissiveness, self-renunciation and subjection of will, as Emerson's second wife did.

Life was a catch-22 situation also for the single woman. She was socially ostracized, pitied because she "couldn't find a husband," considered flawed in character, ignored as an eccentric. However, some "old maids" preferred their status because they retained their independence and retained the advantage of some legal and economic rights. Property and earnings were theirs to keep and control. But they were handicapped by poor job opportunities and wages.

Most women, poorly educated as were slaves, were blinded to their real situations. Margaret Fuller saw the realities and overcame or struck through many of these barriers. And she did not hide herself or her work as did Emily Dickinson and so many other women from whom we'll never hear.

Though Emerson's path was not a bed of roses either, his was easier, and the mores of the early nineteenth century were not against him. In fact, for men the first half of the nineteenth century was a boom period with so much enterprise that Henry David Thoreau felt pressured to create the remark that it would be glorious to see mankind at leisure for once.

Men were high on expectation, ripe for reform. All around were opportunities for employment, for individual self-fulfillment, for self-satisfaction, for upward mobility. It was the period of our country's most rapid growth, an expansion that would eventually urbanize rural America. Critics termed the times materialistic, exploitative, competitive, speculative.

It was a time when the most imaginative of dreams, the boldest of adventures and the most idealistic of utopias became realities. America was in dynamic change...in antebellum transformation economically, politically, socially, philosophically. America had stood independent on its own feet less than fifty years. The American Revolution had been fought and the Peace of Paris had been signed. Louis XVI had been guillotined. The French Revolution was concluded. It was evident that all men (not Negroes, Indians or women) were created equal. Liberty and equality, the rights of man, majority rule were inaugurated. Commonly heard were words about the potentiality of man, the perfectibility of man, the freedom of mankind.

Cities were enlarging. Population was multiplying on both sides of the Mississippi, with the states of Indiana, Mississippi, Illinois and Alabama admitted to the Union. In the North manufacturing was rivaling shipping as solid money-maker. Complete factory villages sprang up, built around the woolen and textile mills which were spanning rivers and falls. In the South cotton was bringing in the dollars. The new look in towns was steam, electricity, and hot blast furnaces. Mass production systems were introduced. Unionization was in the suggestion box.

In 1803 (the year Ralph Waldo Emerson was born) the United States paid France $12 million for the purchase of Louisiana, a province which stretched from the Mississippi to the Rockies. It was the same year that Ohio was admitted to the Union. The following year President Thomas Jefferson made it possible for two young explorers, Meriwether Lewis and William Clark, to take an overland expedition to find a water route from the Missouri river to the Pacific. Trappers and traders and missionaries and bold frontiersmen crossed the Great Plains. The government decreed land grants and allowed slaves to be taken West. Squatters settled onto free acreage where the maxim was "might makes right."

As Sarah Margaret was being weaned and Ralph Waldo was being primed for Harvard, Indian chiefs were given whiskey to entice them to sign treaties surrendering their lands. The Battle of Tippecanoe was fought, and the nation was thrown into the War of 1812, a battle pitched against England over trade and Indian and sailor's rights, a war deplored as a war of conquest.

By the time Sarah Margaret was reading the classics at the age of seven, and by the time Ralph Waldo was entering Harvard at 14, Napoleon had abdicated, and the war was at an end.

The transportation revolution was underway, opening up markets and frontiers. Pennsylvania was building her own roads. Congress was dispensing federal moneys for more construction. Steamboats carrying freight inexpensively were commonalities on rivers. When Sarah Margaret was seven, construction began on the Erie Canal.

When she was nine all America was discussing whether or not Missouri should be admitted to the Union as a slave holding state. When she was ten the Compromise was settled that north of the southern boundary no slaves would be permitted. Admission of the state of Maine balanced the USA to 12 free states and 12 slave states. Immigration from Germany, Ireland, and England was increasing, and immigration spelled cut-rate wages. When Fuller was 15 the Erie Canal was finished, and when she was 16 the first railroad was set on its tracks.

It was the age of the discovery of the use of ether as an anesthesia, the identity of electricity, and there was new research on currents and energies. It was the age of the invention of the daguerreotype, and the camera, the pencil, the sewing machine, the electromagnet, the application of the spectroscope to astronomy, the telegraph, the revolving pistol, the reaper, the vulcanization of rubber, the collapsible metal tube, the use of cans to preserve food, machine-made buckets, and machine tools with interchangeable parts.

There were improvements in the mechanics of printing which led to reduced publication costs and the birth of the penny press. Free public libraries were being supported by taxes. For the first time a paying lecture, debate, and entertainment circuit began to network between lyceums, mechanic institutes and masonic temples. Recreational areas came into development; large wooden hotels sprang up near select beaches for vacationers.

The age was a renaissance for new ideas. The rigid self-denying Puritan theories of John Calvin were being challenged. Dogmas of hell and damnation were being abandoned, as well as ideas of the fear of a God of wrath and the innate depravity of man. The literal interpretation of the Bible was questioned. Though controversy raged, the new clergymen, led by The Rev. Dr. William Ellery Channing and, later, The Rev. Ralph Waldo Emerson, preached self-reliance, independence, spiritual faith and inner strength, that within man himself lay the divine power to determine his own direction, to make change.

Enterprising optimism, staunch individualism and a Jacksonian rugged aggressiveness permeated the air—for white men, young or old, rich or poor, educated or ignorant, American born or foreign born. "Now all things hear the trumpet," Emerson wrote in his essay, "Man The Reformer."

One does wonder what Fuller could have accomplished if she hadn't had to fight against the constrictions of woman's sphere.

One wonders, had she been a man, wouldn't posterity have allotted her deserved space in textbooks? You would know who she was today and your life would have been enriched by her words and actions.

One wonders that if she'd lived another forty years to be eighty—the same span of time Emerson had available to him—wouldn't we be talking of <u>his</u> influence on <u>her</u>?

Why has Margaret Fuller been forgotten?

Reasons have been advanced by knowledgeable persons. For example, Fuller was not a very good writer. She was brilliant in conversation; thus her best vitality is lost to us. Her writing style is too flowery, too old-fashioned, with too many classical references. Her work is too difficult to plow through today. She was an intellect, a literary critic; what she actually <u>did</u> is difficult to articulate.

All this is to some extent true. But the same statements can be made about Plato or Emerson, or any number of male writers whose names are engraved in our minds today. (Some persons might refute statements condemning Fuller's writing because they find what she wrote is brilliant and contemporary.)

Fuller died in her prime—before she had time to complete a large body of work or her best work.

True, yet she had written *Woman In The Nineteenth Century* and had earned world fame. She had been editor of *The Dial Magazine.* She had been a major critic, journalist, and foreign correspondent. We remember many men of equal achievement, many men who have died young. For instance, Henry David Thoreau who passed away two months short of becoming forty-five.

There is also the major fact that Ralph Waldo Emerson, William Henry Channing and James Freeman Clarke, all warm close friends of Fuller's, initiated the perspective and chain of events that has controlled her reputation, has rendered her a marginal position, and largely relegated her out of history.

Let's take a look at Margaret Fuller's reputation today. What is heard or known about her? Is the following story the only thing you have heard?

At dinner with Mr. Thomas Carlyle, Margaret Fuller said, "Mr. Carlyle, I accept the universe!"

Carlyle resounded: "By Gad, you'd better!"

This story perpetuates the myth that Fuller was ridiculous.

But nineteenth century intellectuals on both sides of the Atlantic gloried in such a continuing passionate debate on the explanation of man's relation to the universe.

Emerson asked in his book *Nature* : "Why should not we also enjoy an original relation to the universe?"

Henry David Thoreau wrote in his journal: "That ancient universe is in such capital health, I think undoubtedly it will never die." [20]

The minister/writer/cartoonist Christopher Cranch once joked that even after the talk of the Transcendentalists the universe remained firm on its base.

Have these men, for their statements, been considered ridiculous?

The famed philosopher/humanitarian/architect/scientist Buckminster Fuller, who liked to be called the nearest living relative of Margaret Fuller, sent me copies of the Carlyle/Emerson correspondence to prove that Carlyle had admiration and respect for Fuller. The only proof of the story was that, after she died, Carlyle wrote Emerson that Fuller had "such a predetermination to <u>eat</u> this big universe as her oyster or her egg, and to be absolute empress of all height and glory in it." * [21]

But such stories are never eradicated.

Or have you heard of James Russell Lowell's poem?

All America laughed when Lowell, anonymously, satirized Fuller, along with other writers of the day, in his poem-book, *A Fable for Critics*. It was Lowell's vitriolic reaction because she'd called his verse "stereotyped" and had written that "posterity would not remember him."

In her book, *Woman In The Nineteenth Century*, Fuller had referred to herself as "Miranda." Thus, Lowell picked up on the name:

...But there comes Miranda, Zeus! where shall I flee to?
She has such a penchant for bothering me too!
She always keeps asking if I don't observe a
Particular likeness 'twixt her and Minerva;
She tells me my efforts in verse are quite clever;—
She's been travelling now, and will be worse than ever;
One would think, though, a sharp-sighted noter she'd be
Of all that's worth mentioning over the sea,
For a woman must surely see well, if she try,
The whole of whose being's a capital I:
She will take an old notion, and make it her own,
By saying it o'er in her Sibylline tone,
Or persuade you 'tis something tremendously deep,
By repeating it so as to put you to sleep:
And she well may defy any mortal to see through it
When once she has mixed up her infinite *me* through it.
Miranda meanwhile has succeeded in driving
Up into a corner, in spite of their striving,
A small flock of terrified victims, and there

* Once Emerson wrote in his journal that he had a dream that the world was an apple and an angel commanded he eat it—and he did.

> With an I-turn-the-crank-of-the Universe air
> And a tone which, at least to *my* fancy, appears
> Not so much to be entering as boxing your ears,
> Is unfolding a tale (of herself, I surmise,
> For 'tis dotted as thick as a peacock's with I's)... [22]

The leading critic, Edgar Allen Poe, harshly took Lowell to task for such worthless, unfunny lines, particularly about Margaret Fuller whose genius he claimed did not warrant such invective.

Another story some few people remember concerns Nathaniel Hawthorne who named his Brook Farm heifer after Margaret Fuller. In his notebook he wrote: "She is very fractious, I believe, and apt to kick over the milk pail." The next day he wrote: "Miss Fuller's cow hooks the other cows, and has made herself ruler of the herd, and behaves in a tyrannical manner." And two days later he wrote: "The herd has rebelled against the usurpation of Miss Fuller's heifer; and whenever they returned out of the barn, she is compelled to take refuge under our protection. So much did she impede my labors by keeping close to me, that I found it necessary to give her two or three gentle pats with a shovel."* [24]

Though Hawthorne once recorded having a delightful after-noon conversation with Fuller at Sleepy Hollow[25], he also wrote in the same notebooks, "I was invited to dine at Mr. (George) Bancroft's yesterday with Miss Margaret Fuller; but Providence had given me some business to do, for which I am very thankful." [26]

Brought to full public sensation in 1884 was Hawthorne's vituperative power play and duel jealousy and attraction to Fuller when his son published a new selection of the notebooks in which the great writer slandered Fuller as not having "the charm of womanhood." She had "a strong and coarse nature" and was "a great humbug." "She had stuck herself full of borrowed qualities."

> It was such an awful joke, that she should have resolved...to make herself the greatest, wisest, best woman of the age. And to that end, she set to work on her strange, heavy, unpliable, and, in many respects, defective and evil nature, and adorned it with a mosaic of admirable qualities, such as she chose to possess; putting in here a splendid talent and there a moral excellence, and polishing each separate piece,

---

* Thomas Wentworth Higginson claimed the cow was probably imaginary. [23]

and the whole together, till it seemed to shine afar and dazzle all who saw it. She took credit to herself for having been her own Redeemer, if not her own Creator....[27]

All this was quite the literary scandal at the time. Many were still alive who had personally known Fuller. Many were reading Julia Ward Howe's biography on Fuller, published the year before, which lauded Fuller. Also, Thomas Wentworth Higginson's biography was being brought out, with further adulation.

Yet Julian, the Hawthorne son, blasted that Higginson should have known better. "The majority of readers will, I think, not be inconsolable that poor Margaret Fuller has at last taken her place with the numberless other dismal frauds who fill the limbo of human pretension and failure." [28]

Hawthorne's notebooks further revealed that he had good word from Mr. Mozier, an American merchant and sculptor with whom Fuller and her husband, Ossoli, had lived for a few weeks in Italy. Hawthorne claimed that Ossoli was "half an idiot," "destitute of all manners," "and without pretensions to being a gentleman."

He inferred that Fuller had never written a book of the Italian Revolution. "There appears to have been a total collapse in poor Margaret, morally and intellectually." He said it was a happy destiny that Fuller had drowned: "Providence was, after all, kind in putting her and her clownish husband and their child on board that fated ship." [29]

Hawthorne attacked the Fuller/Ossoli relationship: "I do not understand what feelings there could have been except it was purely sensual." He struck out against Fuller's acceptance of love and loss of her virginity: "...she proved herself a very woman after all, and fell as the weakest of her sisters might."

Fuller's admirers wrote strong public rebuttals. They claimed that Mr. Mozier was known to be a social gossip who probably was piqued because he'd not been invited to Fuller's evening gatherings.

Biographers have explained that when Hawthorne wrote these passages he was projecting his own neurotic fantasies, that it was late in his life and his mind was failing. But Hawthorne's attitudes and charges against Fuller permeate into twentieth century sensibility.

Hawthorne found Fuller's personality so threatening that he could only deal through attack. Imagine the hours he devoted to thinking about Fuller as he created her as a major character in his novel *Blithedale Romance,* published two years after Fuller's death by drowning. It's a book which many, many literary buffs have read over the years because it depicts the Brook Farm utopia. The heroine, Zenobia, is a passionate, assertive, witty, intelligent advocate of woman's rights who drowns herself, unrequited in love.* Some worthy persons also conjecture that the leading figure in *The Scarlet Letter* is also based on Margaret Fuller, because of the out-of-wedlock birth situation.

Besides stories and anecdotes that debunk, there are some classic left-handed compliments that a small minority can recall. The most famous one is Edgar Allen Poe's statement, "Humanity can be divided into three classes...Men, Women, and Margaret Fuller."

Horace Greeley said, "Noble and great as you are, Margaret, a good husband and one or two bouncing babies would emancipate you from a great deal of cant and nonsense."

Fact: Go to the beautiful and famous Mt. Auburn Cemetery in Cambridge, Massachusetts and ask at the desk where you can find Margaret Fuller's monument. The attendant will say, "Margaret *who?*" The clerk will get a list and tell you Margaret Fuller is not commemorated there. You will have to be persistent—after all, Susan B. Anthony was unsuccessful in finding it.[31] Expect the clerk to ask questions of other staff members, to dig deep into files, be confused.

The name Margaret Fuller is today not on the Mt. Auburn Cemetery List of Noted Persons.** Many persons of lesser accomplishment from all over the USA are on it, including many of her lesser known friends and students. Point in fact: Cambridge-born Margaret Fuller often relaxed from her intense work by

---

* Henry James on Fuller's effect on Hawthorne: "It is safe to assume that Hawthorne could not on the whole have had a high relish for the very positive personality of this accomplished and argumentative woman, in whose intellect high noon seemed ever to reign, as twilight did in his own. He must have been struck by the glare of her understanding, and, mentally speaking, have scowled and blinked a good deal in conversation with her. But it is tolerably manifest, nevertheless, that she was, in his imagination, the starting point of the figure of Zenobia." [30]

** Send for pamphlet, "Role of Distinction—List of Noted Persons Interred in Mount Auburn Cemetery, 1831-1952." Indeed, Fuller is not interred at Mt. Auburn because her body washed out to sea, but she does have the attractive four foot high monument next to her son in the Fuller family plot. Her high achievement is worthy of mention, with an explanatory footnote, in the Roll of Distinction.

strolling through the wide green paths, and her mother saved assiduously for months to be enabled to erect a monument to her daughter in the Fuller family plot. But the Cantabrigian proprietors of Mt. Auburn Cemetery do not choose to anoint her in their printed materials.

People who have never heard of Margaret Fuller and suddenly want to know something generally go straight to the encyclopedia—probably the *Britannica*. But if you were living when Julian Hawthorne published his scandalous words, you would have found no information there because Margaret Fuller was not included.

Fuller was not in the *Encyclopedia Britannia* until 52 years after she'd died, until the 10th edition, 1902. But if you looked her up then, you would never have learned that Margaret Fuller had written a popular, revolutionary book because her most significant accomplishment is not mentioned in the 10th, 11th, and 12th editions of this encyclopedia which young and old use as the most indisputable reference tool available. This omission consigns Fuller to a figure of lesser stature.

Each of those editions, from 1902 through 1929, uses the exact same wording and, in an article spanning more than half a page, downgrades the worth of Fuller three times:

> (1) ...while in Boston she also conducted conversation classes for ladies in which philosophical and social subjects were discussed with a somewhat over-accentuated earnestness.
> (2) ...(she) applied herself to her companion as the sponge applies itself to water.
> (3) ...Smart and pungent though she is as a writer, the apparent originality of her views depends more on eccentricity than either intellectual depth or imaginative vigour. [32]

These distortions color the attitudes and thinking of all who read the article.

Furthermore, *through four editions* Fuller's death was listed as June 16, 1850. Fact: Fuller died on *July 19*, 1850.

Thus, I suppose we can half forgive writer Odell Shepard for affirming in *Pedlar's Progress* that Bronson Alcott received the terrible news of Fuller's death in *June* of 1850.[33] Inaccuracies can be amusing.

Happily in the 14th edition of the *Encyclopedia Britannica*, 1929, some mistakes are corrected! Fuller is only referred to as "eccentric." Other denigrations were omitted! Her famous book is given space! She is even praised!

Her death date remained incorrect.

In 1974 her death date was correct!

In the latest and current 15th edition—which represented the results of a 45 year revolutionary overhaul and revision—*shades of the 1902-28 editions*, Fuller again gets harshly slammed:

> Margaret Fuller's career was one of endeavor to overcome many obstacles, a few of her own making. Emotional and impulsive, she was capable of the most intense attachments; her friends, however devoted, often found her too demanding in personal relationships. Hawthorne thought her a pretentious humbug, and James Russell Lowell responded in kind to her criticism in his *Fable for Critics*. Because her books and columns are diffuse in organization and undisciplined in style she has not survived as a notable writer; but she is remembered for the brilliance and erudition of her person and personality. [34]

All this is in the *Micropedia* section, the volumes devoted to subjects of lesser importance, while Ralph Waldo Emerson is allotted page after page of double column in the *Macropedia* section where major matters are considered. Do you think Emerson had no vulnerability?

Thus, encyclopedia users today obtain an unjust impression of Margaret Fuller. Students are not attracted to choose this unnotable woman to read, study or think about.

How is it that we read Margaret Fuller died on *July 16, 1850*, in the first sentence of a chapter devoted to her, page 286 of *Transcendentalism in New England*? Immediately we formulate suspicions of Boston-born Transcendental-advocate minister-writer Octavius Brooks Frothingham *who was well and alive* on the day of Margaret Fuller's death. His book, published in 1876 and republished in 1965, has been praised as a classic, used by researchers into this century as "indispensable."*

Just a *minor* editorial or printer's error?

Another amusing inaccuracy surfaces when Regis Michaud writes that the chosen editor of *The Dial* was Fuller "...who had shown her mettle in Horace Greeley's workshop on *The New York Tribune.* "[35] Fact: Fuller's "mettle" on the *Tribune* was yet to come. First she worked on *The Dial,* later on the *Tribune.*

O. A. Firkins tells us in *Ralph Waldo Emerson* that the death of Emerson's son "shot a troubled ray through the torn soul of Margaret Fuller in her stormy exile." Firkins assuredly refers to Fuller's revolutionary period in Italy—that was her "stormy exile." Fact: Fuller was nearby in Cambridge and Boston when Waldo Jr. died on January 28, 1842. She was seeing Emerson frequently.

Omissions, inaccuracies, distortions, denigrations abound in the books.

Opinions, impressions, reactions magnify and crucify.

Thus we have in the Pulitzer Prize winning *Main Currents in American Thought,* published in 1927, the brilliant and ever fascinating Vernon Louis Parrington, whose work is still so valued that it is considered "an institution," summing up Fuller's life and work as "failure." He starts out by lauding her to the hilt, mentions right off that she overcame obstacles that her male contemporaries never had to deal with—his words are so magnanimous as to nearly take your breath away—but, never fear, he is soon damning: "...she wrote nothing that bears the mark of high distinction either in thought or style." [36] He claims that she should have married early and turned her excessive energy into domestic channels.

Well, do you want to give much thought and attention to a failure?

One wonders why Parrington bothered about her.

Parrington downgrades Fuller's abilities as a critic: "...she plunged vigorously into the work of criticism, never perhaps very successfully, certainly never with high distinction. Her judgments were penetrating and individual...but she was not a notable critic.

---

* At least Frothingham devotes an entire chapter to Fuller, which is more than he did for Henry David Thoreau whom he completely left out in this book on Transcendentalism.

A fine craftsmanship she never attained. A light touch she could never command." [37]

Either Parrington lacked a sense of humor, or he never read Fuller's pungent criticisms. Also, he failed to see that Fuller was one of America's first who boldly formulated standards for literary criticism.

At least he gave her the compliment of a chapter—except for Harriet Beecher Stowe no other woman was so deserving. But Parrington's perspectives are one-dimensional.

We can see how all this filters down through the years.

In 1936 we have eminent historian Henry Steele Commager coining the term "muscular-minded" [38] to describe the intellect of Margaret Fuller. In the '60's he is labelling her "high-flying," [39] and "aggressive" [40] while Emerson is "Olympian." On another page he stated Fuller "looked to Emerson" [41]—as though she took her guidance in all matters Transcendental from him, whereas in reality Fuller always stood her own ground.

Commager uses the trick of mentioning Emerson before mentioning Fuller's name as editor of *The Dial,* thereby the reader is led to believe that Emerson was the more influential.[42] "*Poor Margaret,*" Commager wails, she *toiled,* she *pled,* she *labored* on *The Dial,* while "Poor Emerson" reluctantly but *bravely* took it on,[43] (italics mine), and thereby the reader conjures the impression of a bedraggled Fuller and a brave Emerson. It's your laundered male perspective showing through, Mr. Commager, and it only reveals a part of the truth.

More mis-information occurs when Henry Steele Commager states that Fuller rejected some of Thoreau's poems *without mentioning Emerson's rejections of Thoreau's poems.* [44] He states that Fuller "made" *The Dial* "a vehicle for women's rights" *without discussing her insertion of a wide variety of articles, most of which were written by men whose opinions did not coincide with hers.* [45] He misstates that Fuller was "attracted" to Brook Farm,[46] in fact, a *member* of the Brook Farm community,[47]—no wonder so many knowledgeable people today think she played a large part in that experiment.

Commager wrote that "Emerson was glad to contribute to her (Fuller's) biography." [48] This is a mis-truth, though in later writings Commager showed he'd finally read Emerson's letters and realized that Emerson begrudged working on Fuller's *Memoirs.*

You can weep tears because of an up-to-date vision which misunderstands, mispromotes and bends the truth so as to preserve the eternal powerlessness of Margaret Fuller. On the front page of the *N. Y. Times Sunday Book Review* on the publication of Fuller's letters in 1983, we have reviewer James R. Mellow state in the first line that "Margaret Fuller was *mistress* to her age." [49] (Italics mine.) Right away you have to doubt his veracity. He calls her life "abrasively intellectual," "stereotypical." She was "a figure of literary anecdotes." Later on he writes: "In her relationships with men, Fuller unfortunately had a penchant for younger men of an intellectual stamp."

But these belittling unauthenticies are inconsequential compared to how the traditional perspective has treated Fuller in textbooks that are required reading in schools. After all, it is from textbooks that you and I develop our first impressions of history— and these are the books which give sons and daughters and their sons and daughters their impressions of our living present which becomes their past.

The treatment of Fuller in textbooks can be described very quickly because most have omitted mention of her. Some have allotted her a sentence or a paragraph.

Do not feel guilty or apologetic if you have never heard of Margaret Fuller.

Were you one of thousands who ordered through the Book-of-the-Month Club the *Oxford History of the American People* by the distinguished Samuel Eliot Morison (published by Oxford University Press in 1965)? If so, you did not read about Margaret Fuller for in this people's history she does not exist. The woman's movement barely exists. This is the typical treatment in history books.

Maybe in school you had some study assignment that brought you to that classic reference, the Twayne Publishers' 1973 edition of *Ralph Waldo Emerson* by Warren Staebler. If so, you would have thought that Margaret Fuller played a *minor* role in Emerson's life and nineteenth century America —and probably you would never have remembered her for out of 243 pages she is mentioned slightly *three times* – even though Staebler's editors knew full well the importance of Fuller—that is, if they were aware of their house book list—for nine years earlier they had brought out *Margaret Fuller* wherein the author, Arthur W. Brown, judged that Fuller was worthy of study because she was an appendage to Emerson. (The book is discussed later.)

Even so, in Staebler's book, with three mentions, Fuller wins the most space of any of the women, over Ellen, wife #1 of one year, who is alluded to *twice,* and over Lidian, wife #2 of 47 years (who outlived Emerson), who is afforded a few brief moments as "she" or "her" and whose name is used *once.*

Women may well cry out with clenched fist at the injustice of Staebler who, with a sweep of a sentence, wiped out Fuller's unpaid labor as editor of *The Dial,* giving her deserved credit to Emerson:

> It was his Transcendentalism which brought Emerson into a journalistic relation with society through *The Dial,* a periodical which he helped found in 1840 and for two years edited, until its death in 1844...[50]

Staebler failed to mention that Fuller was first editor in full charge for the first two years.

Suppose a man had first held that *Dial* chair. Do you think Staebler would have disregarded him?

The Dial would probably have never existed without Margaret Fuller. Emerson assisted her as editor. He appointed her because he did not want to be editor. With great reluctance Emerson later took over the helm and only then because no one else would volunteer. All this was well known to Transcendentalists—in fact, the painter/poet/minister Christopher Cranch gently poked fun by sketching a carriage, representing *The Dial*, in which Emerson sat in the back seat and attempted to give *back-seat* directions to Margaret Fuller who was *in the front holding the reins* of a Pegasean team. (The drawing has apparently been lost.)[51]

All of these facts are in the earlier book on Fuller brought out by Staebler's publisher, 1964, (except for the story about Cranch's cartoon). Thus, Staebler and the publishers drop Fuller and the other women out of history.

Here's another way to gloss over women's worth—and we take this outdated, old fashioned 1895 textbook just as a random typical example of what has and does happen across the century. Henry A. Beers in *Initial Studies in American Letters* leads students to believe that Emerson was the primary editor of *The Dial* by listing his name first, before Fuller's, and by stating that Emerson's and

Thoreau's work on the journal was superior: "The most lasting part of its contents was the contributions of Emerson and Thoreau." [52] This is hardly fair, not only to Fuller but to a few others who broke their backs to meet deadlines.

In Beer's text there are three inaccuracies on the one page on Fuller: that she was activated in the temperance cause, that she "took part in the Brook Farm experiment," that her "collected writings are somewhat disappointing, being mainly of temporary interest." In summation he denigrates: "Her strenuous and rather overbearing individuality made an impression not altogether agreeable upon many of her contemporaries." [53] Echoes of that tightheld male perspective that males think needs perpetuation.

If you are after some facts on the history of American journalism and go to the New York Public Library Annex to research early newspapers, you'll likely receive in hand *American Journalism, A History of Newspapers in the United States through 250 years, 1690 to 1940,* because this is the special reference in the head librarian's office which he will kindly lend you. In this, the author gives decided credit to George Ripley for his literary work on the *New York Daily Tribune,* even though Ripley followed in Fuller's footsteps as literary editor, and even though Fuller's work usually took lead spot on the front page with her byline or with an ✳ which the reading public knew to be her identifying mark, while Ripley's work appeared on pages six or eight without a byline. Note also that Fuller's years as a critic, as a foreign and a war correspondent are completely disregarded. The author allots Fuller two years on the *Tribune* staff whereas she worked for about five:

> The *Tribune* was the "first daily to establish a regular department for reviews. This work was under the care of George Ripley for some thirty years. Margaret Fuller was a distinguished member of the staff for two years; she had gained a wide reputation by her feminist and transcendental writings."

George Ripley gets all the credit again in his biography, *George Ripley,* Houghton Mifflin & Co.'s 1882 American Men of Letters Series. Note that the first and last sentences are not correct.

...a literary department (on *The New York Tribune*) was not as yet organized. Subsequently, the man (Ripley) made the place, but for several years the journal, afterwards so distinguished as a tribunal of letters, took a modest position. There was at this time no such thing as systematic criticism of literary work in the daily paper.

It is excruciatingly painful to realize how in book after book the work and influence of our country's most significant women are positively shunted aside. The rage rises as you page through the volumes. You find you're on your feet, out of your great easy-chair, pacing the floor, nerves shaking.

The double whammy comes when you realize that many women's studies books—whether written and edited by men or women—follow this same pattern of slight or omission when it comes to Margaret Fuller. They often cite the English Mary Wollstonecraft who pioneered for equal rights in England and the French Germaine de Staël who did the same in France, but they forget America's Margaret Fuller. According to these books, the women's movement in America begins with the Seneca Falls Convention of 1848, even though Fuller's 1845 famed book, *Woman In The Nineteenth Century,* helped to lay the groundwork for this Convention by generating extensive awareness and public discussion of women's issues throughout the USA and abroad, and even though the women leaders at the Convention recognized Fuller in a spoken tribute and drew upon many of her ideas for the Declaration of Sentiments.

The president at the first national women's rights convention in 1850 in Worcester, Massachusetts (to which Emerson turned down an invitation to speak), had looked forward to the leadership of Margaret Fuller. Furthermore, Elizabeth Cady Stanton, Susan B. Anthony and Matilda Joslyn Gage dedicated their classic *History of Woman Suffrage,* to Margaret Fuller along with other inspiring ground-breakers.* For years to come Fuller was praised in speeches by such women as Ernestine Rose, Paulina Wright Davis, Sarah Grimke, Ann Preston, and by men like Wendell Phillips.

---

* Lucretia Mott, Harriet Martineau, Lydia Maria Child, Sarah and Angelina Grimke, Paulina Wright Davis and others.

You have by now surmised that a great deal of the blame for the dastardly disregard of Fuller can be laid at the doorstep of the three men who wrote Fuller's *Memoirs,* published 1852, which has served for over a century and a half as basic research material for writers.

Emerson was urged by William Henry Channing and Horace Greeley to collect materials on Fuller and to edit the book. But Emerson doubted the value of this work. He did not want to take time out from his regular routines, and he did not want the burden. He questioned in his journal if Fuller was worth a memoir and later wrote that "Margaret & Her Friends must be written but not poste haste."

But Horace Greeley kept pressing for manuscript. So Emerson incorporated the help of William Henry Channing and Sam Ward, who backed out, after which he secured James Freeman Clarke. Emerson's earliest idea was to suppress Fuller's literary criticisms of "the boys." To Greeley: "...whatever is printed, let the notices (her criticisms) of Longfellow and Lowell be omitted...There is no need to repeat the wounds." [54]

A little later Emerson made it plain to Sam Ward that Emerson would be the decision-maker as to the book's worth. Perhaps it should be burned:

> ...it will not be quite plain what (the editor) is to take and what he is to leave of these manifold threads, some pale coloured, and some glowing. The personalities are essential;—leave them out and you leave out Margaret. It would be prudentest for all parties to abdicate any part in the matter,—all but the editor—& make up their hearts to take their fate from his discretion. But when he has finished his task, I think, he must bring it to our jury to decide whether it shall go to the press, or to the flames. [55]

Burning, not shredding, was the common method of destroying papers—Margaret Fuller burned some of her father's papers, Nathaniel Hawthorne burned his wife's love letters, the Emerson daughter burned some of her mother's correspondence.[56]

A year later Emerson, still in the beginning stages of the work, continued to have doubts about commemorating Fuller:

> Elizabeth Palmer Peabody ransacks her memory for anecdotes of Margaret's youth, her self-devotion, her disappointments.... These things have no value, unless they lead somewhere. If a Burns, if a de Staël, if an artist is the result, our attention is pre-engaged, but quantities of rectitude, mountains of merit, chaos of ruins, are of no account without result—'tis all mere nightmare; false instincts; wasted lives.
>
> Now, unhappily, Margaret's writing does not justify any such research. All that can be said, is that she represents an interesting hour & group in American cultivation; then, that she was herself a fine, generous, inspiring, vinous, eloquent talker, who did not outlive her influence; and a kind of justice requires of us a monument, because crowds of vulgar people taunt her with want of position. [57]

Happily, the memoir did get printed. But what happened to Fuller?

Observe the unforgivable, unfathomable act of allotting ten lines in the entire two volumes to Fuller's greatest achievement, her book, *Woman In The Nineteenth Century*. In this paragraph Fuller is quoted as to how she finished the work, and *that is all.* There is some attempt to add a few paragraphs which show her aims in writing this book but these are discursive, not pointedly relevant. There is no discussion as to the importance of the book, its content, its public or press reaction, or how it sold. In fact, *there is just no other mention of her book.*

The second sin is that Fuller's power and force as editor of *The Dial* is buried in two and one half pages. As top executive, she launched every single one of the Transcendental reformers-writers, giving each a sustaining platform on which to speak. That achievement alone should have placed her name among the immortals of literary history.

Her front page reporting on *The New York Daily Tribune* is equally difficult to find and absorb.

But these little omissions by some of our country's most brilliant men are just for starters.

Contemporary scholar Robert Hudspeth, who has done the painstaking work, has given us the most vivid and complete account:

Finally, eighteen months after her death, Fuller got her memorial: *Memoirs of Margaret Fuller Ossoli* was published in two volumes by Phillips, Sampson and Company of Boston in February 1852. In many ways the book was a notable success, for her biographers were talented men. Choosing from a wealth of sources, they picked informative letters, lively passages from journals, and solid essays. They knew exactly what they were doing, and they did it well. No one, then or now, has been in a position to match their selection. They were interested in showing Fuller's mind, and so they printed her remarks on books; they wanted to capture her personality as they experienced it, so they let her speak for herself, which is exactly what she would have wanted.

But Channing, Clarke, and Emerson so bowdlerized and manipulated their evidence as to ruin a splendid book. The *Memoirs of Margaret Fuller Ossoli* is a mess. Given their complex set of motives, the editors created a version of Margaret Fuller that is distorted by their own points of view. They had to repress her sexuality, her quarrelsomeness, her brooding sense of incompleteness, and her increasingly radical political point of view. On the one hand, they did what any biographer must do: they created a personality they understood. On the other, they did not have a complete record to work with, for they knew nothing about the Nathan episode and little about her European life. Finally, the mid-nineteenth century did not share our insistence on the sanctity of texts. For them, private writing was just that: private. No one saw a problem in excising paragraphs written in haste or sickness, in pique or passion; no one doubted the need to protect the reputations of surviving friends and acquaintances. The evidence, though, suggests another level of creation, an attempt to make Fuller intellectually safer and sexually acceptable, her marriage normal, her son legitimate.

One can hardly overemphasize the effects of that memorial both in its accomplishment and in its harm. Because it was constructed from manuscripts many of which were later lost or destroyed and because it was written by three close friends, each of whom understood a part of Fuller's personality, the book cannot be ignored. No later work save Thomas Wentworth Higginson's *Margaret Fuller*

Ossoli went beyond its function as a memorial to a dead friend: it created a mythic Margaret Fuller.

Emerson and his friends recognized the value and richness of her letters for a predominant portion of what they used comes from them. Unfortunately, they often did not like (consciously or not) what they found, and so they set about "improving" upon the situation. What they did varied from editor to editor. Clarke played a smaller part than the other two, probably because of his late arrival on the scene. Most of his section is based on Fuller's letters to him and on her autobiographical account of her childhood. Few of the original letters he presented survive, so it is difficult to assess his editing.

Emerson, like his coeditors, omitted almost all names, failed to distinguish between passages of letters and journals, and used snippets taken completely out of context, but he does appear to have quoted accurately, if we can generalize from the few comparisons we can make between surviving holographs and his copies or his published versions. He routinely altered punctuation and slightly modified wording, but otherwise remained reasonably faithful to the text. Channing created the most serious problems for his readers. He had the troublesome last half decade of Fuller's life to cover, and he seems to have been most willfully capricious in handling the manuscripts. His section of the *Memoirs* is a briar patch. People are misidentified: separate letters are silently joined together; letters are joined to *Tribune* essays; and Fuller's language is often drastically changed.

We can make these observations on the book: (1) Almost no letters are intact. As a result, Fuller sounds tiresomely serious; her voice is habitually literary and self-searching. A reader of her letters as they were written quickly sees that she mixed her criticism and her Romantic self-scrutiny with family matters, gossip, and business details. The whole tone changes if she is presented through nothing but excerpts. (2) She appears in the *Memoirs* to be consistent in her attitudes, but in fact she could be quite one woman to one correspondent and another to a second. Without knowing to whom the letters were addressed, a reader cannot know which Fuller is speaking. (3) The promiscuous mixing of letters and essays obliterates the rhetorical situation that prompted the writing. The public and private voices merge into one continually public Margaret Fuller. (4) The shattered chronology in the *Memoirs* (misdatings are common; much of the material is undated) obscures the growth of Fuller's mind and personality. (5) The necessary gaps created by the limited number of sources created large blind spots in the *Memoirs:* no hint, for instance, of her love for Davis, Ward, or Nathan. (6) Fuller's childhood letters were not used in the *Memoirs,* so her early life is recreated only by her adult autobiography, which, while revealing, is an *ex post facto* account that tells us more about Fuller's adulthood than about her childhood.

Thus the very format of the *Memoirs* created limitations about which we can do little, for many of the original documents were destroyed. The editors often scissored a passage from a letter and then pasted it onto a sheet at the appropriate spot in their text. Emerson ruefully said later that these sheets came back from the typesetter so soiled as to be ruined. A portion of the manuscripts in Channing's possession was later given to Higginson for his biography. He, in turn, left most of them to the Boston Public Library. The sad evidence of the physical abuse still exists: letters have whole paragraphs blotted by gobs of purple ink; other letters are cut into halves or quarters; editorial changes are written over Fuller's writing.[58]

Thus was Fuller treated in her first biography.

It is sad but fascinating to see how a reputation can be slanted across a century.

Let us look not only at books on Fuller but at works about Ralph Waldo Emerson. Since Emerson was Fuller's colleague, intimate friend and first biographer, references to her in his biographies will give insight and help to establish her significance—or insignificance.

As a secondary issue and as a comparison, we will note other significant relationships, mainly Emerson's two wives, as typical of how women, the wives of eminent men, are treated in historical reference. The line of thought may best be followed if the story is told chronologically.

After *Memoirs*, Fuller's brother, Reverend Arthur, decided to keep alive the genius of his sister by publishing collections of her writings. First, he made poor selections. Secondly, he tried his limited best to appease American rumor mongers by exonerating her from her infamous European affair by twisting her into some kind of Christian fanatic or domestic saint.* Nothing more need be said about Rev. Arthur.

There is no other work on Fuller for some thirty years.

We move straight to Emerson's first biographer. George Willis Cooke cleverly left the influence of the women out of *Ralph Waldo Emerson*, 1881, by stating that he did not intend to cover Emerson's personal life but nevertheless his manuscript would be "biographical because light may be thrown upon his books by the events of his life." [59]

Thus, he included a three-page description of Emerson's house and garden, a 15 page description of Emerson's male ancestors, *two pages* of which describe the character of his father and *one sentence* of which describes his mother because Cooke wrote: "How shall a man escape from his ancestors?" Since Cooke practically left out Emerson's mother, his wives and other female friends, Cooke must have felt a man could easily escape women.

In the minor space he allots to Fuller, he denigrates, distorts, and misses the truth. I quote only a few of the most blatant statements:

Cooke Statement

(Emerson) had very reluctantly made her (Fuller) acquaintance, distrusting her sharp personality, and having a horror of those 'intense times' she was reported to have occasionally. [60]

Fact

Emerson had difficulty in relating to people. He was especially uneasy around women.

---

* *At Home and Abroad*, ed. A. B. Fuller. Boston: Crosby, Nichols; London: Sampson Low, Son & Co., 1856. *Life Without and Life Within*, ed A. B. Fuller. Boston: Brown, Taggard, & Chase; New York: Sheldon; Philadelphia; J. B. Lippincott; London: Sampson Low, Son & Co., 1860.

Cooke Statement

...they (Emerson and Fuller) soon became friends, though they never found full sympathy in each other. [61]

Fact

A complex hot/cold relationship developed. Cooke was either blind to it or ignored it.

Cooke Statement

In her (Fuller's) aspirations after a higher life for women he (Emerson) fully shared, entering earnestly into sympathy with all enterprises having that object in view. [62]

Fact

Emerson was not particularly supportive of women's issues. He repeatedly wrote out derogatory views of women in his journals. He refused invitations to speak at Women's Conventions until 1855 after the efforts of the early feminists had launched women's issues into the popular public limelight. He supported the vote with doubletalk meant to discourage women. "I do not think it yet appears that women wish this equal share in public affairs." [63]

English writer Alexander Ireland met Fuller in England when she was an acclaimed celebrity, but his book *Ralph Waldo Emerson, A Biographical Sketch,* 1882, includes reports of male friends, personal male recollections, letters and records of speeches from and of the men. Ireland was a friend of Emerson's; they'd met in Edinburgh in 1833 and he coordinated Emerson's 1847 lecture tour. He made a surface try to include the women, but could not do an adequate job because it is apparent that he did not have access to the Fuller/Emerson correspondence. He apparently made no effort to dig anything up.

The next year, 1883, taking a giant step forward, Julia Ward Howe, Fuller's contemporary and friend, offered the first commendable critique of writings and criticisms with her biography, *Margaret Fuller.* But Howe didn't have access to all the papers, did leave out many vital details, did blur time sequences, did not dig deeply into the Fuller/Emerson relationship, and looked through the nineteenth century style of rose-tinted glasses. From today's hindsight, the book is good for what it is, but limited in scope.

The next giant step was taken the next year by Thomas Wentworth Higginson in *Margaret Fuller Ossoli,* 1884. He had the many papers and letters. Thirteen years younger than Fuller, his elder sisters had played with Margaret, and he had played with her younger brothers. Later the families were connected by the marriage of Fuller's sister. He was always a supportive, generous friend.

Higginson took the bull by the horns to disestablish the triumvirate of Emerson-Channing-Clarke by stating in his introduction, "If my view of Margaret Fuller differs a little from that of previous biographers, it is due to the study of these original sources. With every disposition to defer to the authors of the *Memoirs,* all of whom have been in one way or another my friends and teachers, I am compelled in some cases to go with what seems the preponderance of written evidence against their view." [64]

Higginson portrayed a more complete Margaret Fuller personality, but her stature is continued to be underplayed. Had Higginson (as well as other biographers) been discussing a man's life and work, he would have placed greater importance on accomplishments and their lasting effects.

That same year the colorful Oliver Wendell Holmes—who constantly satirized Emerson's philosophy—brought out his book, *Ralph Waldo Emerson,* 1884. Holmes had been a classmate of Fuller's, had known Fuller all her life, had known Emerson for over 50 years, he must have known Emerson's wife, Lidian. But in his book Margaret Fuller gets about three mentions, including one short paragraph about how Emerson wrote her *Memoirs.* (Of course, the full story of what Emerson did in the *Memoirs* is left untold.) In customary fashion, Emerson's father gets three pages and Emerson's mother gets one paragraph. Emerson's first wife gets two sentences, one for marriage and one for death. His second wife gets nine lines plus another mention on a later page. It's amusing to see how Holmes (inadvertently?) confused events of the second marriage by leaving out the marriage date, inserting mention of nuptials <u>before</u> Emerson gave the Second Centennial

Address in Concord, whereas in actuality Emerson *delayed* the wedding in order to deliver this Address. Admittedly, this is minor, but it probably wasn't so minor to the bride who waited.

Holmes wrote at length about Emerson having to work hard to support a family: "He was called to sacrifice his living, his position, his intimacies...and he gave them all up without a murmur.... He gave up a comparatively easy life for a toilsome and trying one; he accepted a precarious employment, which hardly kept him above poverty...."[65]

This was not the case at all. Emerson had grown up poor and was, as an adult, enabled to pursue precarious employment, the work of his choice, because of substantial income from both wives.

Holmes cites passages which show Emerson speaking out *for* women, once at the 1855 Boston Woman's Rights Convention at which his remarks were actually an attempt to keep the species in her place. Thus does Holmes see and write about what he wants to see and write about.

It was James Elliot Cabot who next manly raised the pedestal of Emerson and shovelled the load of dirt that helped to bury Margaret Fuller and the other women in history.

Cabot, a major, major, major, major Emerson biographer, was his literary executor. He was such a close friend that son Edward wrote of him as being "younger brother." Cabot was no dummy. He held the chair as lecturer on Kant at Harvard.

Cabot came to Concord to work on the papers and presented them to Emerson for final revision and stamp of approval. He stayed at the house; he saw him the day he died. He had access to all of Emerson's files and to the family. He had to have read Emerson's letters to Margaret Fuller, Caroline Sturgis, etc. He had to know Emerson's relationship to his wives and his attitude towards Margaret Fuller.

Cabot wrote *A Memoir of Ralph Waldo Emerson*, 1887, in an easy going, conversational style which obviously purports to reveal the full, intimate portrait of the man, the people, events and influences that shaped his life and thought, but in this book he:

(1) Denigrated the character of Margaret Fuller.
(2) Distorted Fuller's relationship with Emerson.
(3) Slighted the work of Fuller on *The Dial*, indicating that Emerson did all the work, that Emerson did Fuller a favor by becoming editor himself.

(4) Dismissed the first marriage in one sentence: "In September he got married." [66] Thus, he avoids the use of Ellen's name. He never wrote one sentence about their married years together, and never once explained what it was she died of or that Emerson's desolation over her death was a factor in his resigning his pulpit and leaving for Europe.

(5) Slid over the Lidian/RWE engagement and marriage in a likewise sparse manner: "Two days after the Address he drove to Plymouth and was married." [67] He never adequately described Lidian, her background or story. Thereafter, he carefully avoided mention of her, so we get less a picture of wife Lidian than we do of friend Margaret Fuller. Cabot did include letters Emerson wrote to Lidian, but only one of intimacy and this is left unexplained so the reader is left puzzled.

(6) Overlooked the intimate influence of Caroline Sturgis (and Anna Barker), all of whose correspondence he had to have seen as literary executor.

(7) Failed to mention Emerson's work on Fuller's *Memoirs,* let alone the black-inking job.

(8) Slanted the income factor so as to seem that Emerson worked hard to pay the bills.

(9) Skipped facts of Emerson's slowness and failures in childhood and youth.

The following is just a brief selection of many sections that will illustrate Cabot's treatment of Fuller:

Cabot Statement

...She flung herself against him, as Mr. Higginson says, again and again, often with a pain of recoil....

Fact

Emerson gave Fuller just cause to pursue his friendship. Emerson was so fascinated with Fuller that he cultivated the relationship until she died. He continued to invite Fuller to Concord, continued to write her long and warm letters. In Europe he invited her to Paris to be with him. He invited

Fuller to live with him and Lidian; then to live across the street from him.

Cabot Statement

It was really not his fault; she did not hold the key, and he could not open himself to her.

Fact

Emerson did not give "the key" of his inner self to anyone. He was not fully "open" to any man or woman other than, perhaps to a limited extent, his first wife, Ellen. This was his own flaw though Cabot manages to make it Fuller's.

It is exciting to lay hands on a commemorative written by Emerson's son, Edward, (out of print) to be read by the select group of Concordians who were personally acquainted with his father. This would surely offer personal anecdotes of his father, mother and family life that no one else could possibly know about. Excitement is added when we read in son's introduction: "I pass lightly over (his public life and works) to show to those who care to see, more fully than could be done in Mr. Cabot's book consistently with its symmetry, the citizen, the villager and householder, the friend and neighbor." [68]

It is hard to believe that Edward could forget the women who surrounded him as he was growing up, but he did. *Emerson In Concord* is practically devoid of mention of his mother, sisters, or "Aunt Lizzy" (Elizabeth Hoar) who was so often in the Emerson home that she was considered part of the family, who was there for every birth including his own. There is one exception—he did write well about Aunt Mary Moody Emerson, his great aunt, whom he saw less frequently, whom he knew only in her later years. His mother—who is referred to as "Mrs. Emerson" or "his wife"—gets about six brief mentions in 259 pages, with no personal descriptions or anecdotes. Ellen Tucker gets about three mentions and Margaret Fuller gets three. Edward probably couldn't remember Fuller, but he must have seen his father's and his mother's journals and correspondence and heard talk of her as well as Tucker and Hoar.

We see the tight knitting of "The Old Boys' Network."

This is why women need to develop their own network.

In 1895 a woman who had attended and recorded a year's worth of Fuller's Conversations published her account in *Margaret And Her Friends*. The notetaker was Caroline Healey Dall who had been nineteen when she transcribed in 1841. Dall was clearly an intelligent and unstereotypical woman who in some ways admired and patterned her own life on Fuller's independence and feminism but, as she stated, between them there was a "speedy difference that the world would have called a quarrel." [69] She lambasted Fuller for her love of power and sarcastic unequal insensitive treatment of herself. Both were strong, highly motivated women with minds of their own. Reading in her private journals we begin to suspect Dall's personal biases, possibly caused by her young age. Her book, *Margaret And Her Friends*, does offer inconclusive and limited insight into Fuller, as it largely concerns this circle of women who attended the Conversations.

The name of Franklin B. Sanborn often comes up in discussions among well-read people today because he came to know Concord and its people after Fuller died and he wrote about everyone he knew. He taught the Emerson children in his youth and he wrote personal anecdotes of his good friends in his 1903 book, *Personality of Emerson*—which was for sale, interestingly enough, the same year Julia Ward Howe edited and brought out *Love Letters of Margaret Fuller, 1845-46*. The collected letters caused quite a sensation because so few had been aware that Fuller had quietly been enamored of a young immigrant German Jew while she'd worked in New York—and this erotica came out less than twenty years after Hawthorne's slurs had caused tongues to wag. After such dizzying proof, Fuller could be nothing but a siren.

But you wouldn't have found one negative or positive about Margaret Fuller if you'd read Sanborn that year, for he too disregarded the women in his 130 pages, except for details that most interested him, i.e., Mrs. Emerson serving tea to himself and some ten friends, and Mrs. Emerson showing them about her garden, giving them bouquets. You'd think he could and would describe what Mrs. Emerson looked like since he'd been around her so often, what she said, what she did, etc., but no.

To give you an idea of Sanborn's mentality—because he is often quoted as an expert in discussions on Transcendentalism—I offer these tidbits: He mentions how Sarah Ripley was an "excellent housekeeper, "[70] when she was, in fact, more erudite than most men, though he does not mention that. He does mention taking Greek lessons from her, but offers us no particulars of his sessions with this "excellent housekeeper."

Sanborn also thinks to proffer the information that Caroline Sturgis' eyes "were a compliment to the human race,"[71] and chooses to enlighten us with the juicy morsel (which I've so far never seen verified in other print material) that Elizabeth Hoar had been "intimate" with William Ellery Channing before she became engaged to Emerson's brother, Charles.[72]

Assuredly, Sanborn had heard much of Margaret Fuller, and he could have written stories about her, but only in his biography on Henry David Thoreau does he choose to repeat how she rejected Thoreau's literary output for *The Dial.* Sanborn must have "forgot" that Fuller published two of Thoreau's pieces in the first *Dial.*[*] He "forgot" that, when Fuller rejected, she first praised and asked for a rewrite and re-submission. Of course, he left out the insignificant fact that Emerson repeatedly asked Thoreau to revise. A few times Emerson even changed Thoreau's poetic words—once they had quite a literary hassle. Sanborn, evidently, could never conceive of the fact that both Fuller and Emerson knew so well—that the 23 year-old Thoreau's early work could have used some improvement. Sanborn "forgot" that Fuller criticized everyone, even the seven-year-her-senior Emerson, in the hope of bringing forward the best. He "forgot" that Emerson in turn criticized and re-wrote Fuller's work. Sanborn could think of nothing else to say about Fuller.

Rather solid unsentimental stuff is in *Ralph Waldo Emerson* by George Edward Woodberry (1907). But look what he does to Fuller—the words in *italics* are mine to emphasize how his word choices serve to malign:

> (Fuller) had energy of the heart as well as of the head, and she tried *with much desperation, it would appear, to win into his intimacy.* His responses to her, pleading the barriers of his nature and retiring into dumbness as his assigned state in this world, as well as his remarks about *the chills with which her presence at times affected him when she unhappily sought to thaw*

him, sufficiently disclose the situation. "She ever seems to crave," he says, "something I have not, or have not for her;" and again, "She freezes me to silence when we promise to come nearest." He was brought much into relations with her through their joint interest in *The Dial, and he was as serviceable to her* as his opportunities allowed, as he was to every one; and he joined in writing her memoir after her death. On her part *finding the impenetrability of the defence, she had long desisted from the attack.* [73]

Emerson's journals and letters prove how distorted is Woodberry's viewpoint. As for the other influential women in Emerson's life, Woodberry runs stereotypically, barely mentioning both wives twice. Again, Margaret Fuller gets the most space— about 25 lines in a 197 page book. The Emerson children get a sizeable space, and there are several lengthy mentions of Emerson's walks in the woods.

In 1915 Oscar W. Firkins demonstrated by far the greatest imagination (and jealousy?) in executing his venom upon the character of Margaret Fuller, by now 65 years dead. Firkins could not have known Fuller. The three pages devoted to Fuller in *Ralph Waldo Emerson*—outnumbering the pages he allotted to the wives—spring to life in an otherwise sedate biography as he sarcastically peppers them with his personal brand of mudslinging. (Note: The *italics* are my method to make sure you catch exactly how he does it.)

The remarkable person who impressed strongly the New England of her time and who *had the knack of eliciting homage from people far abler and worthier than herself* remains, at our present distance, one of the most *inscrutable of personalities.* There is no lack of clear-cut, even of poignant and mordant, traits, but in the wilderness of attributes *one searches fruitlessly for the evasive character: one chases Margaret through Margaret in vain.* It is not merely that *her published writings give slight indications either of intellectual eminence or of that temperamental vigor which would account for her mastership in conversation, that they suggest, indeed, either an astonishing good luck* with her contemporaries *or a grave misadventure* with posterity,—but that even the 'Memorabilia' which the piety of her friends has compiled do not convey the impression which they obviously wish to convey. Poor Emerson conducts his share of the "Memoirs" in a ceremonious, laborious fashion, praising assiduously, compunctiously, almost apprehensively, bringing up each new excellence for the inspection of the skeptical reader with an anxious, "There, will that convince you?" Then he tells us that she wore her friends "like a necklace of diamonds about her neck," that she resembled "the queen of some parliament of love," and that "persons were her game," his intentions are quite void of malevolence. He does not withhold the evidence of her *childish superstitions (she was given to omens and amulets), of her colossal egotism* which found in America, after painstaking search, *no intellect comparable to her own, of her social veracity which skirted the magnificent and the brutal* in the same breath.

The facts half persuade us to believe that Miss Fuller, in spite of *a coating of masculinity,* was at heart profoundly feminine, that *she was indeterminate,* that *she shared in that receptiveness and plasticity,* that dependence on suggestion, which has been attributed, *more or less plausibly,* to women so eminent as George Eliot and George Sand. The *possession of considerable ability and of a masterful temper* enabled her to *screen this formlessness and instability* from the eyes of her admiring contemporaries. *Her abilities, her pursuits, her ardors, were loose, versatile, and tentative.* Hence that splendor in conversation—that response to the mood, the hour —which had *too little reality or stability to be capable of transference to the printed page or of reproduction in spoken words on the ensuing day. She was not a strong soul with speech as its appropriate and exclusive vehicle; she was a formless being to whom speech imparted the semblance of organization.*

These criticisms apply chiefly to the New England Margaret, the prodigy and prophetess, the precocious child *pampered* on Latin and Greek...In Italy, 1847-50, *she was lucky both in fortune and misfortune.* She won the love and accepted the hand of Angelo Ossoli, a *plain,* affectionate, and faithful young man, in whom these merits lost none of their worth by association with an Italian courtship....

That Emerson admired and valued Miss Fuller is certain, *though,* as often happens in commerce, *the stock curiously shrank when tested by an inventory; whether he "liked" her is another question. Mr. Cabot is probably right in supposing that "a*

> *slight shudder qualified the pleasure with which he welcomed her* *visits to his house.* " She taught him nothing and the stimulus she *brought was rather galvanic than intellectual.* But Emerson's gratitude for stimuli included *even influences that were momentarily perturbing or distracting,* and he was always magnetized by the gift of spontaneous and eloquent conversation. In animated speech the air seemed tremulous with possibilities; a dialogue held for him the palpitant interest of a seance. Margaret Fuller and other such *dominating personalities* affected him with a vague but kindling sense of power, like the rush of unseen wings in the air, or the reverberation of the tread of hurrying multitudes in a remote street. [74]

In the 1920's it's not surprising to find an attempt at a Freudian analysis of Margaret Fuller. Katharine Anthony's *Margaret Fuller: A Psychological Portrait,* miserably fails, even seen through the Freudian eyeglass. The writer superficially totals Fuller to be a mature adolescent instead of a woman of great intellect. She misses on many points, jumbles time sequences, and the conclusions are no longer valid.

We will pass swiftly over the 1929 *Emerson, The Wisest American,* by Phillips Russell because he drew a straight farrow *in summary only* and he also only denigrated Fuller slightly. But, so you'll know from whence he comes, he continued the cycle of giving more play to the Concord house than to Lidian. About her he wrote, "She was one of the modest, unexacting women of her time, readily obscuring herself that her husband might grow." Then, after writing that Emerson drove his bride to Concord in a chaise, he drops her as though her story were concluded, happily ever after—which was by no means the case.

In 1930 Margaret Bell managed to prove again what the earliest biographers told us, that Fuller's life was more important and more interesting than her accomplishments. Her work on *The Dial, The Tribune,* and her famous book are barely mentioned in *Margaret Fuller* . There are also minor inaccuracies and omissions. It is unfortunate Eleanor Roosevelt wrote an introduction which emphasizes that Fuller was a role model because she sacrificed herself for her family and because she possessed "the humility which was prepared to sit at the feet of any great men or women."

These qualities, which today would freeze women into a fearful paralysis, were revered in that 1930 era but, frankly, the latter comment is just in no way true of Margaret Fuller.

That popular writer who everybody used to read, Van Wyck Brooks, who thrived on lively colorful detail, who bent the truth to make it more interesting, who tried to get at the heart of every character he wrote about, who wanted history to be so alive that it read like fiction, fuzzied up things quite a bit. In eight lines in *Life of Emerson* (1932) he covered the Ellen Tucker courtship, engagement, and marriage. Also, he connected it in the wrong time sequence, inserting the liaison after Emerson left the Second Church, not before. He wrote so off-handedly that he made the second marriage to Lidian seem like an accident. Lidian's engagement got one sentence on page 60. The marriage got one sentence on page 61. How Emerson and Lidian travelled to their home in Concord got another sentence on the same page, *but* the description of the house got three pages, half of 61, all of 62 and 63 and part of 64. Next, on the bottom of page 64, comes a description of the Emerson daily routine, including (I assume for posterity's sake) the story of how Aunt Mary put the new bride in her place with this remark: "You must remember, dear, that you are among us, but not of us."

Next, on page 65, Brooks gave Aunt Mary another page; thus, Aunt Mary seemed the one and only woman in Emerson's life.

Astoundingly, a Frenchman who'd lived in America gave the Fuller/Emerson relationship an entire short chapter and came mighty close to the truth in *Ralph Waldo Emerson, The Enraptured Yankee*, 1934 .

Questions: Where did Regis Michaud get his facts? How is it that a Frenchman is the first to state the truth and the realities?

Answer: He must have read Emerson's and Fuller's journals and the letters. The journals and the letters reveal the story. Unfortunately, Michaud then lets us down. He denigrated Fuller by repeatedly calling her "malicious" and "poor Margaret." He gives us a miniscule portrait of Lidian, wife #2 of 47 years. He even referred to her incorrectly as Lydia—incorrectly because in marriage she was always Lidian.

But it is with a sense of relief that author Mason Wade, just before World War II, presented at long last a refreshingly clear, fairly balanced, highly readable Fuller biography, *Margaret Fuller:*

Whetstone of Genius (1940). Perhaps now people would take note and give Fuller her earned place in history.

This did not happen.

As the war broke out Madeline Stern issued another lengthy volume, *The Life of Margaret Fuller* (1942), for early teenage reading evidently, which unfortunately pictured Fuller as a paragon of innocence.

The distorted images are mirrored into mid-twentieth century references used today as "Bible." That is to say, Ralph L. Rusk.

What has been considered the definitive Emerson biography is Rusk's, *The Life of Ralph Waldo Emerson*, published in 1949. It is highly detailed, unquestionably good but, amazingly, Rusk has ignored and brushed over the complexities of the Fuller/Emerson/Lidian/Sturgis/Hoar/Barker/Ward relationship *even though he well knew the extent of it* since ten years earlier he had included correspondence from both of them in his gigantic *6 volume* undertaking, *The Letters of Ralph Waldo Emerson*, 1939. In the few sentences Rusk gave us of Fuller, he did exactly as the Old Boys' Network proscribed. Just some examples of the many innuendoes can be shown:

Rusk Text

Margaret Fuller was a gadfly who stung people to action.[75]

Fact

Fuller was an intellectual who wasn't afraid to speak her mind. She often influenced others to take needed action.

Rusk Text

In the spring of 1842 (Emerson) paid a new installment of his debt to Margaret by aiding her escape from the floundering Transcendental magazine, *The Dial*.

Fact

With great reluctance Emerson took over the editorship of *The Dial*, only after he'd made a search for other editors. He did not want the job because it took too much of his time and energy.

Rusk Text

Margaret, having broken away from New England, had already run through her New York period and was now hopeful of absorbing the essence of Europe. [76]

Fact

Fuller was not a flighty socialite who would "run" through her "New York period." This is a belittling choice of words. Note that Rusk did not write that Emerson had "run through his Southern period" when he went to South Carolina for his health.

In 1957 Faith Chipperfield vowed to explore the heart of Fuller, but *In Quest of Love* is easily dismissed because what we have is a fictionalized account with imaginative dialogue to sugar-coat the reality, assumably in order to appeal to readers of novels.

This leads us directly to esteemed and popular former-Harvard professor of American Literature, Perry Miller, mentioned in the opening anecdote concerning Fuller's arrogant egotism. Though *Margaret Fuller, American Romantic* (1963) is largely excerpts from Fuller's writings, Miller's capsule notes have been often quoted. He judged Fuller as of *minor importance.* He evaluated her letters and her *Tribune* reviews to be more enduring than her famed book, but they did not "quite add up to a coherent or really consistent literary personality." [77] Failing to give credence to women's issues, he claimed that *Woman In The Nineteenth Century* was "feminist *propaganda,*" was "actually a *slight* contribution to the campaign for 'women's rights.'" [78] (Italics mine.) "Memorable" as the book might be, "it is full of wearisome digressions, and excursions into fantasy and murky dreams and the thread of discourse is frequently lost." He commented that, because she wrote it quickly,* "the reader must run an exhausting course beside the galloping filly." [79]

With relish Miller detailed her appearance as angular and "monumentally homely," which she was not, her hair was "stringy," which it was not, her costume was "bizarre," which it was not, and in her Conversations "she put on grand performances both of scorn and of indignation," which she did not. [80] He twice inferred that she was suicidal which is a point on which some high caliber scholars would take exception. Miller could never get beyond the the male perspective—Fuller was always "mounting her assault onto (Emerson)." [81] The "strange" Fuller/Emerson relationship was a short-term dalliance: "Mr. Emerson's healthful, even pulse had permitted him for a brief time, around 1840, a series of epistolary flirtations..." [82] She "hardly knew what she wanted;" she was "foredoomed to defeat." [83]

Women readers see through Miller's biased perspective when they read in his *The American Transcendentalists* that everyone laughed at Margaret Fuller's Conversations, which were for ladies who "*aspired* to be Transcendental luminaries," (emphasis mine) and then states that these women were "lacking in humor." [84]

With the year 1964 came the Twayne Publisher's book, *Margaret Fuller,* (mentioned earlier as the one editors at Twayne ignored). This scholar, Arthur W. Brown, built his entire premise on the fact that the woman on which he chose to devote hours upon hours of research was nothing but an appendage to Emerson...a lesser spirit. She was profitable to study only because of Emerson's determined efforts to know her.

There is solid good in Brown's book—(don't pay any attention to his statement that Fuller was not anxious to fall in love in Italy)—but who can be inspired to read beyond the first sentence: "Wakeful and restless as Fancy, the life of Margaret Fuller is a promise of great things never to be fully accomplished." [85]

In 1969 Joseph Jay Deiss' *The Roman Years of Margaret Fuller* held Fuller up to good advantage and he painstakingly delineated in depth for the first time her European struggles. But were later writers influenced to regard Fuller with more respect?

---

* Fuller did not write her book quickly. The article had already been written and published in *The Dial.* She revised and expanded it during seven weeks at Fishskill, and did additional manuscript polish while in New York and beginning work on *The Tribune.*

There are two 1970 Emerson biographers. August Derleth attempts in *Emerson Our Contemporary* to give lip service to Fuller (happily he calls her attractive), but he fails to hone in on the important relationships.

But it is Edward Wagenknecht who "takes the cake" in *Ralph Waldo Emerson, Portrait of a Balanced Soul*, 1974. Almost every reference to Fuller can be disagreed with—there is not space to include them all. Here are a few of the most blatant:

Wagenknecht text

Except with those whom she could dominate comfortably—and Emerson was not dominatable by man or by woman—Margaret's personality was abrasive, and many besides Emerson felt it so. His first impression of her was decidedly unpleasant. "Her extreme plainness,—and a trick of incessantly opening and shutting her eyelids,—the nasal tone of her voice,—all repelled; and I said to myself, we shall never get far." [86]

Fact

Most men were fascinated by Fuller; most women were admiring. Men who Fuller criticized thought her personality was abrasive. Those who admired her described her favorably. Emerson dominated situations as much as Fuller. Both were strong, each in his/her own way. Fuller often made a bad first impression, then people adored her.

Wagenknecht text

But Emerson had no desire to be her Pyramus (nor yet her Ossoli); neither had he any possible obligation to do so. He endorsed one of her letters, "What shocking familiarity." I am not suggesting that Margaret Fuller tried to seduce Emerson, but sybil though she was, her subsequent history shows that she was also a woman whose most imperative need was to be loved. [87]

Fact

Emerson needed love. Fuller needed love. He married twice, had children, kept himself surrounded by women, wrote ongoing, intimate letters to women other than his wife. It is unfair to "put down" Fuller because she, like other human beings, needed and searched for love.

Wagenknecht text

By 1842 she wrote of her relations with Emerson, "But my expectations are moderate now." Unless he had wished to break off relations with her altogether, Emerson probably handled the whole business about as well as anybody could have done it. [88]

Fact

If either one could be said to have "handled the whole business about as well as anybody," then it was Fuller who did the "handling." She left Emerson in Concord, went to New York, and then went to Europe. In both locations she formed new friendships and relationships with men other than Emerson. In fact, Emerson pursued Fuller her entire life.

Three Fuller scholars in the 1970s brought out books that dignify the name we wish most to promote. They are: Bell Gale Chevigny, *The Woman and the Myth: Margaret Fuller's Life and Writings* (1976); Paula Blanchard, *Margaret Fuller From Transcendentalism to Revolution* (1978); and Margaret Allen, *The Achievement of Margaret Fuller* (1979). These are all excellent, the best to date.*

So at last is Margaret Fuller's reputation exonerated?

---

* In addition, Marie Mitchell Olesen Urbanski advanced a complimentary study of Fuller's book, *Margaret Fuller's Woman In The Nineteenth Century* (1980). And scholar Joel Myerson has done wonders with an extensive bibliography and collections, *Margaret Fuller, Essays On American Life and Letters* (1978), *Critical Essays On Margaret Fuller* (1980), *The New England Transcendentalists And The Dial* (1980). Beginning in 1983 a mammoth work of scholarship was accomplished by the publication of Robert Hudspeth's series of volumes of *The Letters of Margaret Fuller.*

I have searched in vain for new perceptual approach in the two new Emerson biographies. The first is the 1981 Gay Wilson Allen *Waldo Emerson,* which was critically hailed as "monumental" and "the best life of Emerson we have," * "massive, masterly," **   and "meticulous and readable narrative." ***

It is well done, but when it comes to Margaret Fuller there is disappointment.

I find fault not that Gay Wilson Allen does not mention Fuller's achievements, because he does, not because he does not quote significant passages, or relate significant incidents, because he does, *but because* he devotes so little space to the giant role and position Fuller earned and held in nineteenth century America, so little space to her enormous influence on the life and thought of Emerson, because he reduces Fuller with chauvinist wording that in the later half of the twentieth century is unacceptable, because he traces her childhood, young life, and relationships with men in a cursory outline that either denigrates or shows his lack of understanding, because Allen mishandles and is insensitive to the various feelings and ramifications of the Fuller/Emerson/wife triangle situation which he chooses to detail, albeit briefly, and because Allen unforgivably fails to mention how Emerson and the other editors of *Memoirs* distorted her character.

In 1984 John McAleer with *Days of Encounter* has done more damage to Lidian and the feminine sex than have previous Emerson biographers who chose to ignore the women. McAleer considers the women but his recurring rapier thrusts breed hate and viciousness that smells of the eternal competitive threat. He ignores facts, twists others, fails to perceive much that has often been downplayed, and conjectures others. He patronizes Fuller, maligns and makes fun of her and her husband, relates as true the stories in the Hawthorne journal, and he interprets mistakenly— not to mention his denigrating chapter thirty-nine subtitle: "an accomplished *lady* ."

The clue to his type of scholarship comes when we read that Fuller is "a kind of spiritual concubine." [89] This is an unforgiving choice of words. More than once he delineates her as being "sad and listless." No one who understood Fuller could so describe her.

---

* R. W. B. Lewis, *The New Republic,* October 21, 1981.
** *Publisher's Weekly,* August 28, 1981.
*** Paul Zweig, *N. Y. Times Book Review,* November 1, 1981.

He excuses Emerson as being innocent (even surprised) in his attraction towards Margaret Fuller and Caroline Sturgis. "He enjoyed the company of both but was in love with neither. He wrote to them as he did so as not to wound their sensibilities." [90] If you read the letters, there is no way to conclude that Emerson only continued seeing and writing to Fuller and Sturgis over a period of years so as not to hurt their feelings.

McAleer writes as though Emerson had the upper hand, that he "managed" Fuller and cut her off, and that she, in her blindness and foolishness, insisted on pursuing, playing a "double game," and that finally Emerson became "caught up in the life of his family, with Fuller gradually receding from view." [91] His slant, again, is that she was "intoxicated" with Emerson; there is no conception that Emerson could have been fascinated with Fuller. Apparently, it is beyond McAleer's ken of understanding that the reason Fuller "receded from view" was because she chose to turn away from him, because she became disillusioned with Emerson.

To Lidian, McAleer is so patronizing, belittling and denigrating that it is frightening. Time and again he emphasizes her illnesses so as to delineate her as a weak psychotic who tears her hair, wrings her hands, weeps, who in general tries the patience and endurance of the entire family and is deserving of no person's love. He infers she could have been a Salem witch: "Had Lydia made her home in Salem instead of Plymouth, the possibility of witchcraft would have to be considered." [92] In McAleer's interpretation, Emerson laughed at this intelligent woman (not with her) even during the courtship. He states that Emerson treated her as a *lusus naturae*, which means a freak of nature. [93] In another chapter he refers to her as "Gothic." [94] According to McAleer, Lidian, who made domesticity her A#1 top priority, was a bad manager of Emerson's clothing, a bad meal planner and cook, and he conjectures that she had to seek Emerson's advice to write a sensitive letter to Henry David Thoreau who admired her. She was such an aloof, high and mighty, judgmental, ill eccentric that no one could possibly live with her and Emerson was a saint to bind himself to her and to have patience enough to be able to put up with this melancholy psychotic whose illnesses Emerson was convinced were recreational. He claims Emerson described her once as though he "might have been describing a corpse." [95]

Repeatedly, McAleer parallels their relationship with that of William Shakespeare's characters Katharina and Petruchio in *The*

Taming of the Shrew, which is a boisterous, raucous power struggle in which the male wins over and totally subdues the female who outwardly seems happy to be subdued. This inaccurate comparison of the character and nature of the Emerson marriage leads to an entirely mistaken impression. Emerson was not a boisterous man who physically threatened his spouse, and Lidian was not a shrew who counter-attacked.

McAleer quotes Emerson as saying: "The arrows of Fate stuck fast in Lydia." [96] He has taken this quote from the daughter's manuscript of her mother, *The Life of Lidian Jackson Emerson.* [97] But, taking it out of context, he shifts the blame of the remark off of Emerson's shoulders so as to portray Lidian as the fated freak.

McAleer has left out the story of Lidian's childhood and life before marriage. If we consider what she was before marriage and how her life evolved after marrying one of the most eminent men in America, we begin to understand the problem and are amazed that this woman only succumbed to illness, not insanity.

McAleer takes no account of Emerson's attitude toward women in general. Knowing Emerson's views are vital to full insight into the man.

For how many years to come will such insensitive conclusions be perpetuated?

It is only recently that women historians, sociologists, scholars and media persons such as Gerda Lerner, Jesse Bernard, Elizabeth Janeway, Donna Allen, Dale Spender (and others) have raised our consciousnesses (and statistics validate their theories) about the fact that history has been written by and seen through the eyes and experiences and value systems of men. Because those in power see and describe life and culture out of their own experiences and points of view, women's work and accomplishments have been considered unimportant, considered not worth space in books.

It is men who are most often in the power positions, men who define, control, and judge. They decide what the issues are, decide the priorities. They decide what gets printed, who writes it, how it is viewed, what is emphasized, and how it is put into the hands of the public.

It is not that women have not done anything or have not made their voices heard—many women have done much and have raised their voices over the centuries. It is that male writers for the most part have not been interested in the achievements and value systems of women. Women have not had a footing of equality and power.

Why it has taken women so long to become enlightened testifies to the thorough brainwashing that has gone on for thousands of years in every culture in the world. Once there can be an awareness of what has happened, there can emerge new energy to tilt the scales so that a fair balance can exist.

Not only does the traditional perspective cheat women of roots, of role models, of aspiration, of inspiration, but it plays havoc with ideals and values women have held in the past and do hold today and do exist today.

Here's what a committee at The Council on Interracial Books for Children writes:

> Not one history text gives visibility to womankind.
>
> This widespread omission of women is not attributable solely to the sex bias of male publishers, historians and editors. The reasons are more complex. Historians of both sexes have been trained to examine the past through a traditional, male perspective which views history as a chronology of momentous wars, treaties, explorations elections, and so forth. Such a perspective automatically excluded women as they never were generals, diplomats explorers or presidents....
>
> Recognition that women have been as essential to history as to life itself—in more ways than biologically reproducing the workforce—will require a radically different perspective for judging what is, and what is not, important in our past The deeds of those few, upper-class, white males who molded and controlled the institutions of our society will then comprise but one segment of our total history. [98]

As is pointed out, children, youths, and adults tend to internalize the words and attitudes that come out of the media and out of the textbooks which seem to indicate the totality of available knowledge and authority. From the selected views and role models presented to us, we all come to an understanding of the life and culture in which we live. If women and women's issues are allotted narrow and minor space, children, youth and all adults tend to learn that women's concerns and lives are unimportant. Thus women, children and all adults tend to act in ways that affirm an substantiate this untruth. Therefore, woman's self-worth is limited. And humankind loses out. Since women represent the majority of humankind, then over half of human achievement and experience is lost to us if it is not recorded.

What would happen to attitudes and mind-sets if media and textbooks gave as much space to the visions, accomplishments and issues of women, from the perspective of women as are given to the visions, accomplishments and issues of white upper-class males? Wouldn't women young and old be proud of their rootage, proud of their womanhood, inspired to high achievement?

Wouldn't both men and women be enriched, be provided with another view, another approach, another reality?

Wouldn't we begin to maximize human potential?

Wouldn't society as a whole begin to place priority on women's issues, on child bearing, child rearing, work in the home, birth control, abortion, pay scale, absence of day care, disarmament, nuclear freeze, peace, etc.?

The angle of vision that the issues, ideals and values of white upper-class males reflect the life and interests in the entire country is simply not realistic because it is one sided. As the Council points out, there are more people in America than "Man."

Once we women see how the subtleties operate we can begin to throw off our angers, fears, denials, guilts, suppressions, repressions, sacrifices, and search for alternatives that will not bind women or men in straightjackets.

Like the nay-saying Transcendentalists, we can refuse to participate in mind-sets, relationships and situations we feel are not positive. We can involve ourselves in mind-sets, relationships and situations which we consider beneficial.

We can say No to an imposed system which perpetuates the oppression of women and maintains one sex as superior or more powerful or more influential than the other. We can turn our backs on stereotypical role playing and can strive for new models. We can define our identities, find out what is best for ourselves, work out our own value system, judge ourselves by our own definitions, not the definitions that the opposite gender has named for us.

We can begin the process of basing our relationships on the truth, harmony, and divinity that the Transcendentalists advocated (but "not for men only")—as well as on the respect, compassion and equality that is still vitally needed in human relationships today.

For how many decades to come will future researchers/writers keep on assigning significant women like Margaret Fuller a minority role?

Footnotes

Note: Reference below is made to first, the last name of the author, second, the key word of the title, and third, the volume and page number. A detailed list of authors, titles and publishers is to be found in the Bibliography, alphabetized by author's last name.

1. Miller/Fuller/Forward/ix
2. Emerson/Memoirs/II/111-2
3. Higginson/Fuller/202
4. Ibid/202-3
5. Sanborn/Personality of Emerson/49
6. Higginson/Fuller/202
7. Frothingham/Transcendentalism/300-01
8. Woodberry/Emerson/66-7
9. Fuller/Life Without and Life Within/"Emerson's Essays"
10. Holmes/Emerson/93
11. J. Hawthorne/Hawthorne & Wife/I/293-4
12. Emerson/Memoirs/I/322
13. Beers/Initial Studies/79-80
14. Stanton/History of Suffrage/I/81
15. Firkins/Emerson/52
16. Howe/Reminiscences/58
17. Quoted Kendall/American Heritage/Founders Five/34
18. Dall/Margaret/35
19. Frothingham/Transcendentalism/301
20. Thoreau/Week
21. Emerson/Correspondence with Carlyle/213
22. Lowell/Poetical Works/IV/62-64
23. Higginson/Fuller/179
24. Hawthorne/Notebooks/II/4/April 13-16, 1841
25. Hawthorne/ Notebooks/II/85
26. Ibid/ I/ 221
27. J. Hawthorne/Hawthorne & Wife/I/261

28. J. Hawthorne/*Weekly Transcript* (a newspaper)/Dec. 31, 1884
29. J. Hawthorne/Hawthorne & Wife/I/259-262
30. James/Story & Friends/80
31. Harper/Susan B. Anthony/1/131
32. The Encyclopedia Britannica/10th Edition/Vol. II/11th Edition/Vol. II/295-6/and 12th Edition/Vol. II/295-6
33. Shepard/Progress/443
34. The Encyclopedia Britannica/15th edition/1974/353-4
35. Michaud/Emerson/72
36. Parrington/American Thought/426
37. Ibid./432
38. Commager/Theodore Parker/55
39. Commager/Search/145
40. Ibid./127
41. Ibid/171
42. Ibid./145
43. Ibid./154
44. Ibid./155
45. Ibid./156
46. Commager/Living Ideas/454
47. Commager/Era of Reform/43
48. Commager/Parker/152
49. Mellow/New York Times Sunday Book Review/June 19, 1983/front page
50. Staebler/Emerson/41
51. F. Miller/Cranch/vii/36, 60-61
52. Beers/Initial Studies/109
53. Ibid./108
54. Emerson/Letters/IV/225-6
55. Ibid./IV/231
56. Emerson, Ellen/Editor: Carpenter/Life of Jackson Emerson/ xiv
57. Porte/Emerson In His Journals/429
58. Reprinted from *The Letters of Margaret Fuller, Volume I: 1817-38* (pp. 61,2,3), edited by Robert N. Hudspeth. Copyright © 1983 by Cornell University Press. Used by permission of the publisher.
59. Cooke/Emerson/v
60. Ibid./122
61. Ibid./122

62. Ibid./123
63. Quoted, Ibid./125
64. Higginson/Fuller/4
65. Holmes/Emerson/372
66. Cabot/ Emerson/ I/146
67. Ibid./I/236
68. Emerson, Edward/Emerson/1
69. Myerson/Dall-Reminiscences/Harvard Bulletin/419
70. Sanborn/Emerson/68
71. Ibid./109
72. Ibid./111
73. Woodberry/Emerson/95
74. Firkins/Emerson/82-5
75. Rusk/Emerson/252
76. Ibid./310
77. Miller/Fuller/135
78. Ibid./xii
79. Ibid./136
80. Ibid./xvii
81. Ibid./108
82. Ibid./xvii
83. Ibid./52-53
84. Miller/Transcendentalists/101
85. Brown/Fuller/17
86. Wagenknecht/Emerson/132
87. Ibid/134
88. Ibid./134
89. McAleer/Encounter/404
90. Ibid./ 330
91. Ibid./407
92. Ibid./202
93. Ibid./215
94. Ibid./405
95. Ibid./215
96. Ibid./215
97. Emerson, Ellen/Editor: Carpenter/ Life of Jackson
    Emerson/ 69
98. Council on Interracial Books/Stereotypes/103

Bibliography

Allen, Gay Wilson, *Waldo Emerson*. Penguin Books, The Viking Press, 1981.

Allen, Margaret Vanderhaar, *The Achievement of Margaret Fuller*, University Park and London: The Pennsylvania State University Press, 1979.

Anthony, Katharine, *Margaret Fuller, A Psychological Biography*. New York: Harcourt, Brace and Howe, 1920.

Baym, Nina, *Woman's Fiction, A Guide to Novels by and about Women in America, 1820-1870*. Ithaca and London: Cornell University Press, 1978.

Beers, Henry A., *Initial Studies in American Letters*, Flood and Vincent. New York: The Chautauqua Reading Circle Press, 1895.

Bell, Margaret, *Margaret Fuller*. New York: Charles Boni Paper Books, 1930.

Blanchard, Paula, *Margaret Fuller From Transcendentalism to Revolution*. New York: Delacorte Press, Seymour Lawrence, 1978.

Brooks, Van Wyck, *Emerson And Others*. New York: E. P. Dutton & Co., 1927.

Brooks, Van Wyck, *The Life of Emerson*. New York: Dutton, 1932.

Brown, Arthur W., *Margaret Fuller*. New York: Twayne Publishers, United States Authors Series,1964.

Cabot, James Elliot, *A Memoir of Ralph Waldo Emerson*, 2 vols. Boston: Houghton Mifflin Co., 1887. Also, AMS Press, New York, Second Printing, 1969, Reprinted from a copy in the collection of Northwestern University Library, From the edition of 1887, Cambridge.

Chevigny, Bell Gale, *The Woman and the Myth.* New York: The Feminist Press, 1976.

Chipperfield, Faith, *In Quest of Love.* New York: Coward McCann, 1957.

Commager, Henry Steel, *The Era of Reform, 1830-1860.* Malabar, Florida: Robert E. Krieger Publishing Co., 1982.

Commager, Henry Steel, *Living Ideas In America,* edited and with commentary. New York: Harper & Brothers, 1951.

Commager, Henry Steel, *The Search for a Usable Past and Other Essays in Historiography.* New York: Alfred A. Knopf, 1967.

Commager, Henry Steel, *Theodore Parker, Yankee Crusader.* Boston: Beacon Press, 1936.

Cooke, George Willis, *Ralph Waldo Emerson: His Life, Writings, and Philsophy.* Boston: James R. Osgood and Co., (Fifth Edition), 1882. Also, Norwood, 1975.

The Council on Interracial Books for Children, Racism and Sexism Resource Center for Educators, *Stereotypes, Distortions and Omissions in U. S. History Textbooks.* New York, 1977.

Dall, Caroline Healey, *Margaret and Her Friends or Ten Conversations with Margaret Fuller upon The Mythology of the Greeks and Its Expression in Art.* New York: New York Times Co. Boston: Roberts Brothers, 1895. Reprint: Arno Press, 1972;

Deiss, Joseph Jay, *The Roman Years of Margaret Fuller.* New York: Thomas Y. Crowell Company, 1969.

Derleth, August, *Emerson, Our Contemporary.* London: Crowell Collier Press-Collier-MacMillan Limited, 1970.

Emerson, Edward W., *Emerson In Concord, A Memoir.* Boston and New York: Houghton, Mifflin and Co., 1889.

Emerson, Edward W., ed., *Journals of Ralph Waldo Emerson.* Cambridge: Riverside Press, 1909-1914.

Emerson, Ellen Tucker, *The Life of Lidian Jackson Emerson,* ed. Dolores Bird Carpenter. Boston: Twayne Publishers, 1980.

Emerson, Ralph Waldo, *The Correspondence of Emerson and Carlyle,* edited by Joseph Slater. New York: Columbia University Press, 1964.

Emerson, Ralph Waldo, *Memoirs of Margaret Fuller Ossoli,* ed. Ralph Waldo Emerson, William Henry Channing, and James Freeman Clarke. Boston: Phillips, Sampson, 1852. Reprinted by Burt Franklin, 1972.

Emerson, Ralph Waldo, *The Journals and Miscellaneous Notebooks of Ralph Waldo Emerson,* ed. W. G. Gilman et al., 14 vols. Cambridge, Mass.: Belknap Press, 1960-1978.

Emerson, Ralph Waldo, *The Journals of Ralph Waldo Emerson,* ed. E. W. Emerson and W. E. Forbes, 10 vols. Boston: Houghton Mifflin, 1909-1914.

Emerson, Ralph Waldo, *Letters of Ralph Waldo Emerson,* ed., Ralph L. Rusk, 6 vols. New York: Columbia University Press, 1939.

Emerson, Ralph Waldo, *The Works of Ralph Waldo Emerson,* ed. J. E. Cabot, 14 vols. Boston: Houghton Mifflin, 1883-87.

Firkins, Oscar W., *Ralph Waldo Emerson.* New York, Russell & Russell, 1965.

Frothingham, Octavius Brooks, *George Ripley.* Houghton, Mifflin and Co., American Men of Letters Series,1882.

Frothingham, Octavius Brooks, *Transcendentalism in New England.* First Published New York: G. P. Putnam's Sons,1876. Reprinted, Harper & Row, 1965.

Fuller, Margaret (Ossoli), *The Letters of Margaret Fuller,* 4 Vols., ed. Robert N. Hudspeth. Ithaca and London: Cornell University Press, 1983.

Fuller, Margaret (Ossoli), *At Home and Abroad,* ed. A. B. Fuller, Boston: Crosby, Nichols. London: Sampson Low, Son & Co., 1856. Reprinted by Kennikat Press.

Fuller, Margaret (Ossoli), *Life Within and Life Without,* ed. A. B. Fuller. Boston: Brown, Taggard, & Chase. New York: Sheldon. Philadelphia: J. B. Lippincott. London: Sampson Low, Son & Co., 1860. Reprinted by Gregg Press.

Fuller, Margaret (Ossoli), *Summer On The Lakes.* Boston: Charles C. Little & James Brown. New York: Charles C. Francis, 1844.

Fuller, Margaret (Ossoli), *Papers and Literature on Art, "American Literature; Its Position in the Present Time."* New York: Wiley & Putnam, 1846.

Fuller, Margaret (Ossoli), *Woman In The Nineteenth Century.* New York: Greeley & McElrath, 1845. Reprinted by W. W. Norton.

Fuller, Margaret (Ossoli), *Woman In The Nineteenth Century and Kindred Papers,* ed. Arthur B. Fuller. Boston: John P. Jewett, 1855.

Fuller, Margaret (Ossoli), *Love Letters of Margaret Fuller, 1845-1846,* ed. Julia Ward Howe. New York: D. Appleton, 1903. Reprinted by Greenwood Press.

Harper, Ida Husted, *The Life and Works of Susan B. Anthony.* Indianapolis: Hollenbeck Press, 1898.

Hawthorne, Julian, *Nathaniel Hawthorne And His Wife, A Biography,* Volume I & II. First published 1884. Reprinted Archon Books, 1968.

Hawthorne, Nathaniel, *American Notebooks,* ed. Claude M. Simpson. Ohio State University Press, Modern Language, Assn., 1932.

Hawthorne, Nathaniel, *The Blithdale Romance.* New York: Norton, 1978.

Hawthorne, Nathaniel, *The Scarlet Letter.* New York: Penguin Books, 1983.

Higginson, Thomas Wentworth, *Margaret Fuller Ossoli.* Boston: Houghton, Mifflin and Co., 1884.

Holmes, Oliver Wendell, *Ralph Waldo Emerson.* Boston and New York: The Riverside Press, Cambridge, 1884. Republished, Detroit: Gale Research Library, 1967.

Howe, Julia Ward, *Margaret Fuller.* Boston: Roberts Bros., 1883.

Howe, Julia Ward, *Reminiscences 1819-1899.* Boston: Houghton Mifflin, 1899.

Ireland, Alexander, *Ralph Waldo Emerson: his life, genius, and writings; a biographical sketch to which are added personal recollections of his visits to England, extracts from unpublished letters and miscellaneous characteristic records.* Port Washington, New York: Kennikat Press, 1972. Reprint of the 1882 ed.

James, Henry, *William Wetmore Story and His Friends,* 2 vols. Boston: Houghton, Mifflin, 1903.

Janeway, Elizabeth, *Powers of the Weak.* New York: Alfred A. Knopf, 1980.

Kendall, Elaine, "Founders Five," *American Heritage, The Magazine of History.* New York: American Heritage Publishing Co., Inc., Vol. XXVI. No. 2, Feb. 1975.

Lerner, Gerda, *The Majority Finds Its Past, Placing Women In History.* Oxford, New York: Oxford University Press, 1981.

Lowell, James Russel, *Poetical works of James Russel Lowell.* Boston: Houghton Mifflin, 1904.

McAleer, John J., *Ralph Waldo Emerson, Days of Encounter.* Boston: Little, Brown, 1984.

Michaud, Regis, *Emerson, The Enraptured Yankee.* AMS Press, 1930.

Miller, F. DeWolfe, *Christopher Pearse Cranch and His Caricatures of New England Transcendentalism.* Cambridge, Mass.: Harvard University Press,1951.

Miller, Perry, *Margaret Fuller, American Romantic.* New York: Doubleday & Co., Anchor Books, 1963.

Miller, Perry, *The Transcendentalists, An Anthology.* Cambridge, Mass.: Harvard University Press, 1950.

Moll, Frank Luther, *American Journalism, A History of Newspapers in the United States through 250 years, 1690 to 1940.* New York: The MacMillan Co., 1941.

Morison, Samuel Eliot, *The Oxford History of the American People.* New York: The Oxford University Press, 1965.

Myerson, Joel, *Margaret Fuller, A Descriptive Bibliography,* University of Pittsburgh Press, 1978.

Myerson, Joel, *"Caroline Dall's Reminiscences of Margaret Fuller."* Harvard Library Bulletin 22, October 1974, 414-28.

Parrington, Vernon Louis, *Main Currents in American Thought, An Interpretation of American Literature from the Beginnings to 1920,* 3 vols. New York: Harcourt, Brace and Co., 1927.

Porte, Joel, ed., *Emerson In His Journals.* Cambridge, Mass.: Belknap Press of Harvard University Press, 1982.

Rusk, Ralph L., *The Life of Ralph Waldo Emerson.* New York and London: Columbia University Press, 1939.

Russell, Phillips, *Emerson, The Wisest American.* Bretanno's, 1929.

Sanborn, Franklin B., *Personality of Emerson.* Boston: The Merrymount Press, Charles E. Goodspeed, 1903.

Shepard, Odel, *Pedlar's Progress.* Boston: Little Brown & Co., 1937.

Staebler, Warren, *Ralph Waldo Emerson.* Twayne Publishers, 1973.

Stanton, Elizabeth Cady; Anthony, Susan B.; and Gage, Matilda Joslyn, editors, *History of Woman Suffrage,* 2 volumes. New York: Fowler & Wells, 1881.

Stern, Madeleine B., *The Life of Margaret Fuller.* New York: E. P. Dutton, 1942.

Thoreau, Henry David, *A Week On The Concord and Merrimack Rivers.* New York: Literary Classics of the United States: Distributed to the trade in the U. S. and Canada by Viking Press, 1985.

Urbansky, Marie Mitchell Olesen, *Margaret Fuller's Woman In The Nineteenth Century.* Westport, Conn.: Greenwood Press, 1980.

Wade, Mason, *Margaret Fuller, Whetstone of Genius.* New York: The Viking Press, 1940.

Wagenknecht, Edward, *Ralph Waldo Emerson, Portrait of a Balanced Soul.* New York: Oxford University Press, 1974.

Woodberry, George Edward, *Ralph Waldo Emerson.* New York: Haskell House, 1968, first published 1907.

Woodham-Smith, Cecil, *Florence Nightingale.* New York, London, Toronto, McGraw-Hill Book Co., Inc., 1951.